ON THE DESTRUCTION
AND DEATH DRIVES

ON THE DESTRUCTION AND DEATH DRIVES

André Green

Translated by
Steven Jaron

Edited and Introduction by
Howard B. Levine

PHOENIX
PUBLISHING HOUSE
firing the mind

First published in French in 2010 by les Éditions d'Ithaque
First published in English in 2023 by
Phoenix Publishing House Ltd
62 Bucknell Road
Bicester
Oxfordshire OX26 2DS

Copyright © 2023 by les Éditions d'Ithaque

Authorised translation from the French language edition published by Ithaque

Translated from French and with a Preface by Steven Jaron

Introduction copyright © 2023 by Howard B. Levine

This translation was made possible by the sponsorship of the Boston Group for Psychoanalytic Studies, Inc.

The right of André Green to be identified as the author of this work has been asserted in accordance with §§ 77 and 78 of the Copyright Design and Patents Act 1988.

British Library Cataloguing in Publication Data

A C.I.P. for this book is available from the British Library

ISBN-13: 978-1-912691-64-7

Typeset by Medlar Publishing Solutions Pvt Ltd, India

www.firingthemind.com

Contents

About the author

André Green, French psychiatrist and psychoanalyst, member of the Paris Psychoanalytical Society (SPP), was one of the most pre-eminent figures of the contemporary psychoanalytic movement, both for his theoretical and clinical research and his role within institutions. In 1965, Green became a member of the SPP, of which he was President from 1986 to 1989. From 1975 to 1977 he was a Vice-President of the International Psychoanalytical Association and from 1979 to 1980 a Freud Memorial Professor at University College London. He was elected an Honorary Member of the British Psychoanalytical Society.

He attended Jacques Lacan's seminars between 1961 and 1967, when he definitively broke with him. He then directed a seminar at the Institute of Psychoanalysis in Paris where he invited the great philosophers and authors of his time, including Jean-Pierre Vernant, Michel Serres, Jacques Derrida, Marcel Detienne, and René Girard. A great reader of D. W. Winnicott and a friend of W. R. Bion, he constantly bridged the gap between British, American, and French psychoanalytical research in a spirit of international openness and turned towards the future of psychoanalysis. His theoretical contributions—the dead mother, private madness, the work of the negative, the tertiary processes and the analytic object—opened the way to psychoanalysis beyond neurosis, the hallmark of twenty-first-century psychoanalysis.

Many of his works, such as *Life Narcissism, Death Narcissism, On Private Madness*, and *The Work of the Negative*, are classics of psychoanalytic literature.

About the editor

Howard B. Levine, MD, is a member of APSA, PINE, the Contemporary Freudian Society, and Pulsion, on the faculty of the NYU Post-Doc Contemporary Freudian Track, on the editorial board of the *International Journal of Psychoanalysis* and *Psychoanalytic Inquiry*, editor-in-chief of the Routledge Wilfred Bion Studies Book Series, and in private practice in Brookline, Massachusetts. He has authored many articles, book chapters, and reviews on psychoanalytic process and technique and the treatment of primitive personality disorders. His edited and co-edited books include *Unrepresented States and the Construction of Meaning* (Karnac, 2013); *On Freud's Screen Memories* (Karnac, 2014); *The Wilfred Bion Tradition* (Karnac, 2016); *Bion in Brazil* (Karnac, 2017); *André Green Revisited: Representation and the Work of the Negative* (Karnac, 2018); *Autistic Phenomena and Unrepresented States* (Phoenix, 2023) and *The Freudian Matrix of Andre Green* (Routledge, 2023). He is the author of *Transformations de l'Irreprésentable* (Ithaque, 2019) and *Affect, Representation and Language: Between the Silence and the Cry.* (Routledge, 2022).

About the translator

Steven Jaron is a clinical psychologist and psychoanalyst working at the 15–20 National Vision Hospital and in private practice in Paris. Before studying psychology at the University of Paris-7 and psychoanalysis at the Psychoanalytic Society for Research and Training (SPRF), he obtained a PhD in French and Comparative Literature from Columbia University. His essays have appeared in the *Libres Cahiers pour la psychanalyse, Bacon and the Mind: Art, Neuroscience and Psychology* (Thames and Hudson, 2019), and *Psychoanalysis and Covidian Life: Common Distress, Individual Experience* (Phoenix, 2021) and he is the author of two monographs, *Edmond Jabès: The Hazard of Exile* (Legenda, 2003) and *Christopher Bollas: A Contemporary Introduction* (Routledge, 2022).

Introduction

Howard B. Levine

André Green begins his exploration of Freud's formulation of the death drive[1] by noting that

> We ought not shy away from contending with Freud's most speculative metapsychology, that which at times roils us due to its impression of being inimical to retreating from the paradise of ideas while nevertheless legislating on problems that concern

---

[1] Editor's note: In this volume, we will be using the designation death *drive* rather than death *instinct*. Strachey made an unfortunate choice when he translated *Instinkt* and *Trieb* with the same English word, *instinct*, because for Freud the two terms allude to a different set of connotations. Instincts produce "a hereditary behavioral pattern peculiar to an animal species, varying little from one member of this species to another and unfolding in accordance with a temporal scheme which is generally resistant to change and apparently geared to a purpose" (Laplanche & Pontalis, 1973, p. 214) and have a relatively stable aim and object. (Think here of salmon returning to the specific waters in which they hatched in order to spawn.) In contrast, *Trieb* is meant to convey "the relatively undetermined nature of the emotive force in question and the notions *of contingence of object and variability of aim*" (Laplanche & Pontalis, 1973, pp. 214–215; emphasis added to the original).

our clinical practice at its deepest, for example, when it elevates itself to examining notions as prevalent and fundamental as life and love, as destructiveness and death.[2]

In Chapter 2, speaking of *Beyond the Pleasure Principle*, in which Freud (1920) begins to seriously consider the death drive as a fundamental component of his dual death theory,[3] Green adds:

> The impact of Freud's revolutionary text from 1920 continues to be felt by the analytic community after well more than half a century. What may be said about it? We might summarize the situation as such: "The words have been declined; the thing, on the other hand, in general recognized" … In the writings of those who see themselves as heirs to Freud's legacy, we surely observe, from Ferenczi up through our time, that the central problem of psychoanalysis today is precisely found among varied forms of destructiveness.

Green's aim is to examine in depth, clinically as well as theoretically, culturally as well as within the individual psyche and the analytic process, the status, evolution, and place of the death drive in the writings of Freud and a series of major post-Freudian writers offering

---

The drive is initially somatic and not represented in the psyche in a form that is ideational or directly knowable. It is a non-specific pressure, a "force without meaning" (Levine, 2022). Only later, as it becomes, produces, and/or unites with an ideational derivative that is psychic does it get attached to a specific object and/or set of aims. But in its somatic form, that is, before it is linked to a derivative that becomes its ideational representative in the psyche, it is ideationally unrepresented. Consequently, Eros and Thanatos are perhaps better thought of as metapsychological hypotheses about "something" in the soma that moves towards discharge in a general and non-specified sense as they "bind" and "unbind", rather than as inherent sources of specific desires (love, hate, etc.). The specificity of aim and/or object of desire are attributes of the *drive derivative* and not inherent to the drive itself. The latter furnishes the drive force or pressure to these derivatives, which may then be transformed and become qualified as erotic or destructive in aim (Levine, 2023).

[2] Editor's note: In this Introduction, all unattributed quotations will refer to Green's text in this book. Since the Introduction was prepared from a manuscript prior to production of the actual book, corresponding pagination has not been possible.

[3] Editor's note: see Footnote 1, p. xiii.

us his conclusions—and inconclusions—for our further reflection and exploration. In so doing, he conveys a continued vitality in the Freudian enterprise and an urgency to protect and advance it. For Green, Freud offers a powerful and unique perspective from which to view human psychology, social organisation, and the existential challenge of finding and creating meaning within one's life.

In addition to carefully tracing and commenting upon the evolution of Freud's thought, this volume may be seen as a continuation of Green's struggles to make sense of, and put into perspective, his lifetime of psychoanalytic reflections and clinical encounters; a reckoning that anglophone readers may access and trace beginning with his 1975 *International Journal of Psychoanalysis* paper "The analyst, symbolization and absence in the analytic setting", continuing with *On Private Madness* (1997), *The Work of the Negative* (1999), *Key Ideas for a Contemporary Psychoanalysis* (2005a), *Psychoanalysis: A Paradigm for Clinical Thinking* (2005b), and eventuating with *Illusions and Disillusions of Psychoanalytic Work* (2011).

For many North American, anglophone readers, there may initially be something that feels foreign, uncomfortably old fashioned, or overly theoretical in assigning so much import and giving such credence to the drive concept. However, I suspect that many readers will come away with a new and meaningfully altered sense of why the drives—and certain key, metapsychological formulations—were and remain so central to Freud's thinking and, indeed, to the essential core of psychoanalysis as a venture into the ineffable realm of psychic reality.

Regarding the latter, Green sounds a warning and cautions contemporary readers:

> there is nothing more alien to common sense than an understanding of psychoanalytic theory … psychoanalytic thought repels those who try to assimilate it from the outside in so far as its fundamental postulates and theorems are at odds with ordinary thinking.

Put simply, although epistemologically it is very far from a simple matter, psychic reality is a very different matter than consensually verifiable "social reality". Thus, Freud's conclusions are not to be seen "in relation to some reality which [one] might capture in [their] net".

For Green,

> The aim of the Freudian enterprise … [aspires] without any moralising ambition, to foreground a previously unknown aspect of human psychic reality.

And the drive remains an essential concept in the matrix of Freudian theory. It is

> a primitive organisation on which the ego has no hold and which tends to reproduce itself without actually being related to the repetitive quest for pleasure but aims, according to Freud, at re-establishing a prior state.

Without the concept of the drive and its force, Green tells us, "Freudian thought is mutilated". Freud viewed the drive as a "paramount concept" and "asserted the right of paramount concepts not to be proved". The structure of Freud's metapsychology is built upon a form of theory-building—dual drive theory; Eros and the death drive; binding and unbinding; pleasure principle *vs.* repetition compulsion—that offers psychoanalysts a coherent conceptual metatheory of psychic organisation, development, and function and informs a pragmatically useful model for clinical listening, understanding, and intervention. That is, there is a *clinical* value to Freud's metapsychology.

Psychoanalytic theory is a set of interlocking models and theories that derive both from clinical observation and the need for theoretical coherence and consistency. Recognising the latter offers a rejoinder to Nagel's infamous criticism that psychoanalytic propositions allow for no disproof. It asserts that the verification and "proof" of psychoanalytic assumptions and theories does not necessarily rest with the degree to which they are found to correspond to observable "facts", but lies instead in the extent to which holding certain assumptions allows analysts to function more effectively in the clinical setting. On this point, in regard to the death drive, Green is quite clear:

> When considering clinical practice, whatever theory one holds or has elaborated, in contemporary psychoanalysis it is always a

matter of coming to terms with destructiveness … Freud himself pointed out three illustrative instances of the death drive: the unconsciousness of guilt, masochism, and the negative therapeutic reaction. While these observations are hardly debatable, modern clinical practice adds quite a few others to them.

While sensual, empirical experience may be a sometimes unreliable guide from which to reach conclusions (Bion, 1970), clinical experience does teach us that

> when painful experiences frustrate the pleasure principle and overwhelm the psyche, they result in experiences of unrepresentable destructiveness owing to their all-out, devastating power, that is [both] external and internal. Deadly anxiety and limitless destruction fill the entire psyche … [I]n such cases we cannot speak of regression to a prior libidinal state but it is a matter of comprehensive regression in which destructiveness is unable to face psychic pain, nor put a stop to it … we're closer here to what Pierre Marty terms disorganization than repression … Pleasure is likewise irrelevant here; paradoxically, only *jouissance* reigns. It is uninterpretable; … interpretations remain ineffective over it … [It is as if it were] a cyclone that nothing can stop.

And yet, paradoxically, clinical experience also teaches that there is sometimes some possibility of amelioration *après coup*—containment, rebalancing if not redress—in the living out, making sense of, and finding words to describe the catastrophic chaos and disruption and the defensive organisations that it has required. That is, acknowledging, bearing, and putting into perspective.

The binding counterforce of Eros, appearing under the aegis of the transference relationship, can help marshal a primal drive towards representation, a "drive of reason … not engendered by objects, but that it engenders its own object" (Kahn, 2005, p. 52). This movement was especially recognized by Bion (1962, 1970) in his theory of alpha function and container/contained and was something that I expanded upon in my description of the representational imperative (Levine, 2012, 2022). It stands at the centre of the paradoxical challenge posed by the status of the drives as unrepresented: how to find words to describe and talk about something that in a sense both does and does not "exist", and that to the extent to which it may "exist" is not fully comprehensible or conveyable by thought or language. Bion (1962) spoke at length of the difficulty involved in trying to "approach a mental life unmapped by the theories elaborated for the understanding of neurosis" (p. 37).[4]

Elsewhere, Green (2005a) noted that Freud's (1923) theoretical shift from the topographic to the structural theory marked a change from a theory centred on psychic *contents* (ideational *representations*) to a theory about *process* and the movements needed to tame the unstructured, not yet represented aspects of *the drive*—that is, emotion, impulse, and somatic discharge—within the psyche. According to Green (2005a), the major development in Freud's revision of theory was the change from

> one model, at the centre of which one finds a form of thinking (desire, hope, wish), to another model based on the act (impulse as internal action, automatism, acting) ... the analyst now not only has to deal with unconscious desire but with the drive itself, whose force (constant pressure) is undoubtedly its principal characteristic, capable of subverting both desire and thinking.
>
> (p. 47)

Green (1984) summarised this irresolvable problematic when he reminded us that:

> There was on Freud's part a deliberate choice that psychoanalysis should be a treatment that worked exclusively through speech, through verbal exchange, and that it should manage to deprive itself of any other means ... the crucial question of psychoanalysis remains: how is it that by means of speech we change something in the structure of the subject, whereas what we change does not belong to the field of speech?
>
> (p. 121)

---

[4] For an extended discussion, see Levine (2022).

While Freud's introduction of the death *drive* raises questions about the essential nature of human aggression and destructiveness, it also asks us to consider:

> Is death truly the aim of a drive? Death and the death drive are different things. Death is a fact … But a drive which pushes towards death can by no means be taken for granted. What do mean by this? If we avoid the controversial term of death drive and above all recall that it is a question of (self- and hetero-) destruction, then things become clearer.

Or do they? For Freud, the hypothesis of a drive contains within itself the force and movement towards

> the return to a previous state of life … [as] the blanket aim of any drive.

What sense do we make of this?

> As always with Freud, the introduction of a new concept puts the equilibrium of the whole into question and requires another conceptualization other than that which had prevailed till then.

As far back as the "Project", Freud (1950, p. 297) proposed that the primary function of the nervous system was that of the regulation of tension through discharge; if not total discharge, then at least keeping the tension level optimal and as low as possible. In subsequent writings, he continued to explore whether it was a matter of constancy or complete inertia (the Nirvana principle). What remains constant for Freud throughout his theorising is his attachment to the model of an activity having as its goal the suppression or reduction of the inner tension produced by the stimuli that inevitably follow from our being-in-the-world, alive and sensate.

In 1920, Freud concluded that "the necessity of binding precedes the search for pleasure" and that it is the tenacity of the repetition compulsion that attests to the presence of the death drive. That, and the war experiences, war neuroses, negative therapeutic reactions, and unconscious guilt led Freud to conclude that man bears within himself an element of hatred as well as a penchant for aggression and destruction, and thus for cruelty. *Beyond the Pleasure Principle* attests to the disillusion concerning the belief in pleasure as a guide to life and the construction of the psychic world.

From the vantage point of a later historical perspective—the Shoah, the Gulag, the atomic bombing of Hiroshima and Nagasaki—Green sees in this a penchant for destruction of both life and the *soul* of the designated adversary:

> The destruction of the soul is what any initiative of servitude and domination in war which pits itself against the other—the foreign(er), the bad, and the hated—seeks. There can be no triumph over the other if the other is left to think freely ... What is sought is the surrender of anything which seems to fall under individual will and which is entitled to express difference, the rejection of or opposition to the other.

Returning to Freud, Green reminds us that in assessing our penchant for destruction, hatred, and cruelty, what is crucial is the relative strength, the binding and unbinding of the Eros–death drive pair:

> What is important is the construction–destruction pair, along with its intrication–disintrication correlate. There are in fact two ways of conceiving the death drive. A restricted application which finds justification without too much difficulty ... [in] cases attesting to the uncontrollable aspiration to failure, unpleasure, suffering. Next there are the goals of the Eros–destruction drive pair, an application which is broader and which suggests a novel vision of psychic life.

Regarding that novel vision, Green suggests that Freud gives us two sets of hypotheses. In one, the primal drive is marked by the tendency to return to a prior state of non-tension, non-life (Freud, 1920, p. 38). Hence the connection of the death drive with the Nirvana and Constancy Principles. Freud, however, later recognised the complexity

of this perspective and ultimately acknowledged that there exist pleasurable tensions and unpleasant relaxations.

The other basic hypothesis "posits a vision of simultaneity": that the
life and death drives both exist from the beginning and *ab initio* it is
always a matter of relative weight, binding and unbinding, intrication
and disintrication. This balance is not only constitutional, but is affected
by the quality of primary object relationships at key moments of developmental opportunity.[5] As one reads through Green's careful exposition of
Freud's discussions, one may wonder from a somewhat different perspective, especially in regard to Freud's speculations about the first move from
inanimate to animate matter, if the press towards unbinding of the death
drive isn't reflected in or analogous to the concept of entropy in physics.[6]

Another facet of Freud's thinking that Green brings forward relates
to the role of the superego and our status as social beings. With the formulation of the superego and in his later writings,

> Freud transposes his field of investigation onto society and
> henceforth sees the elective domain of the death drive within it.
> For culture cannot be founded on drive renunciation alone ...
> The field of culture becomes the arena in which are developed
> the most destructive effects of the death drive.

Green's Freud winds up as philosopher, anthropologist, and sociologist
despite himself. All of Freud's later, so-called non-clinical writings—
Totem and Taboo (1912–1913), *Group Psychology and the Analysis of
the Ego* (1921), *The Future of an Illusion* (1927), *Civilization and Its
Discontents*[7] (1930), and *Moses and Monotheism*[8] (1939)—rest upon two

---

[5] In fact, aspects of the work of Ferenczi, Klein, Winnicott, Bion, Bowlby, Kohut,
Loewald, Green, and others may be seen as a corrective that implicates the actuality of
the primary object in the binding/unbinding process and the selection or balancing
out the force of the self and other destructiveness of the death drive.

[6] Entropy is a measure of the degree of disorganisation in a liquid or gas. Left to its own
devices, without the presence of an organising counterforce, entropy tends to increase
over time.

[7] In this text, referred to as *Discomfort in Culture*.

[8] In this text, referred to as *The Man Moses and Monotheistic Religion*.

fundamental pillars: our biological condition as living beings and the quality of the relations of one human being to another.

> Biology and anthropology do not come under the relation to life alone. They must further include—in relation to the mortal and living human being—that which is immortalised by culture. This is what the Freudian reflection on the death drive teaches us.

Along with Freud (1930), Green asks: what then is civilization? His answer is sobering:

> not all ideologies are bearers of peace. They likewise sow death and threaten the most civilised peoples. We are endowed with law in order to limit the damage. But this may vanish from one day to the next in favour of the most obscurantist prejudices. Think of National Socialism and Communism.

While Freud may sometimes assert that "sublimation has surely gained ground" and that there is "the existence of a 'civilizing process' unfolding throughout humankind", history teaches that these processes continue to pale compared to the excitement and pleasure of relatively unmodified drive discharge, jouissance.

> The feeling of happiness derived from the satisfaction of a wild drive motion untamed by the ego is incomparably more intense than that derived from sating a drive that has been tamed.
>
> (Freud, 1930, p. 79)

> men are not gentle creatures who want to be loved, and who at the most can defend themselves if they are attacked; they are, on the contrary, creatures among whose drive endowments is to be reckoned a powerful share of aggressiveness.
>
> (Freud, 1930, p. 111)

Emphasising the problematic role that culture may play in regard to aggression and destructiveness, Green reminds us that:

Culture, far from succeeding in 'humanising' humans, most often fails. Civilisation does not get the better of barbarism … We need only think of the Shoah.

The abolition of private property gave birth to the Gulag and the new order to the extermination camps. The country in which the Statue of Liberty is found put prisoners in chains and torture was practiced in Algeria by the country of the French Revolution … One must not forget that if civilisation condemns violence, war is nonetheless monopolised by the State.

For Green, this leads to a sobering conclusion: Freudian pessimism

is the disillusioning enterprise which, for him, constitutes the aim of psychoanalysis.

To what extent will our readers agree or disagree? More than simply his own conclusions, Green has offered us this extraordinary book as a way station and launching pad towards future evolutions in psychoanalytic thought.

References

Bion, W. R. (1962). *Learning from Experience*. London: Heinemann.

Bion, W. R. (1970). *Attention and Interpretation*. New York: Basic Books.

Freud, S. (1912–1913). *Totem and Taboo. S. E., 13*: 1–161. London: Hogarth.

Freud, S. (1920). *Beyond the Pleasure Principle. S. E., 18*: 3–64. London: Hogarth.

Freud, S. (1921). *Group Psychology and the Analysis of the Ego. S. E., 18*: 67–144. London: Hogarth, 1961.

Freud, S. (1923). *The Ego and the Id. S. E., 19*: 1–66. London: Hogarth, 1959.

Freud, S. (1927). *The Future of an Illusion. S. E., 21*: 5–56. London: Hogarth.

Freud, S. (1930). *Civilization and Its Discontents. S. E., 21*: 64–145. London: Hogarth.

Freud, S. (1939). *Moses and Monotheism. S. E., 23*: 6–137. London: Hogarth.

Freud, S. (1950). Project for a scientific psychology. *S. E., 1*: 295–397. London: Hogarth.

Green, A. (1975). The analyst, symbolization and absence in the analytic setting (on changes in analytic practice and analytic experience)—In memory of D. W. Winnicott. *International Journal of Psychoanalysis, 56*: 1–22.

Green, A. (1984). Winnicott and the model of the environment: Interview with André Green. In: A. Clancier & J. Kalmanovitch, *Winnicott and Paradox: From Birth to Creation* (pp. 119–126). London: Tavistock, 1987.

Green, A. (1997). *On Private Madness*. London: Karnac.

Green, A. (1999). *The Work of the Negative*. London: Free Association.

Green, A. (2005a). *Key Ideas for a Contemporary Psychoanalysis: Misrecognition and Recognition of the Unconscious*. A. Weller (Trans.). London and New York: Routledge.

Green, A. (2005b). *Psychoanalysis: A Paradigm for Clinical Thinking*. London: Free Association.

Green, A. (2011). *Illusions and Disillusions of Psychoanalytic Work*. London: Karnac.

Kahn L. (2005). *Faire parler le destin* [*Speak, Destiny*]. Paris: Klincksieck.

Laplanche, J., & Pontalis, J.-B. (1973). *The Language of Psychoanalysis*. New York and London: Norton.

Levine, H. B. (2012). The colourless canvas: Representation, therapeutic action and the creation of mind. *International Journal of Psychoanalysis, 93*: 607–629.

Levine, H. B. (2022). *Affect, Representation and Language: Between the Silence and the Cry*. London and New York: Routledge/IPA.

Levine, H. B. (2023). A metapsychology of the unrepresented. *Psychoanalytic Quarterly, 92*(1): 11–25.

Translator's preface

Steven Jaron

On the Destruction and Death Drives is a late work, the fruit of decades of thinking and debating one of Freud's most radical and thus controversial concepts. André Green saw it as growing out of *The Work of the Negative* (1993 for the French edition, 1999 for the English edition) and somewhat overlapping with *On Private Madness* (1986 for the English edition, 1990 for the French edition; the essays comprising the two editions are close but not identical) and further leading up to the still later *Illusions and Disillusions of Psychoanalytic Work* (2010 for the French edition, 2011a for the English Edition) (Green, 2011b, pp. 380–381). As he states in the foreword to the second edition of 2010, which this translation follows in form and content, he believed that this book was one of his "most important works" (see p. xxxiii, this volume).

André Green's study is a vigorous defence and illustration of Freud's advances on drive theory in which he asserts the necessity of taking into account not only drive dualism but fundamentally of recognising the psychic reality of the death drive in the individual psyche and across cultural processes. The evolution of Freud's drive theory is made possible by the structural model and, as Green wrote unequivocally in an overview of his own later works, "Qui dit pulsion de mort dit renoncement à la première topique" (Green, 2011a, p. 380). Put in slightly different terms, we as Freudian analysts "cannot speak of the death drive without giving up the first topography". Even now, as he details the growth of Freud's argument during the pivotal decade of the 1920s when "the concept of the unconscious" is *replaced* by "that of the id" (see Section 3.4), Green deplores the fact that some analysts cannot bring themselves to recognise the primacy of "drive motions" over "unconscious representations" and further to fathom the theoretical validity of the death drive, if not its clinical relevance. These points and others, in particular the relationship of psychosexuality to the death drive, are discussed in the pages below. Notwithstanding, while in no way a psychoanalytic manifesto, *On the Destruction and Death Drives* may be read not as a call to arms, but to *thinking through* the repercussions of destructiveness at the heart of the psyche.

He qualifies his conclusion as "tentative" since so little is illustrated by case material demonstrating the destructiveness of the work of the negative in his patients' psyches. This is, he explains, because "I preferred to let myself work over the memory of my experience with them or, in some cases, with those who are still continuing their experience with me, in pursuit of the *Durcharbeitung*" (see p. 113, this volume). The work of memory fosters working-through and the virtual lack of case material—its absence—gives rise to the question of how the destruction and death drives express themselves in the reader's own clinical practice. In other words, as we proceed through the book, we might ponder how, and to what degree, the destruction and death drives operate not only in our patients but further in the countertransferential dynamic. This, in any case, has been my own experience. Notwithstanding, *Illusions and Disillusions of Psychoanalytic Work* provides a series of clinical illustrations of the work of the negative drawn from Green's own practice as well as that of colleagues.

André Green may at times be polemical, but this does not prevent him from writing as a ferryman of ideas transporting concepts from one intellectual horizon to another, in this work across mainly British and French shores. Is the capacity to make the frontiers thinkable somehow related to his origins as a Francophone, Cairene Jew who came to France as a young man? Foreignness appeared integral to his make-up, as he made his home elsewhere. Nonetheless, conceptualising the borderline was precisely what he succeeded in doing as no one had till then. As he wrote in "The borderline concept", "Our experience has shown us that the limit between madness and sanity is not a line, but a vast territory in which no precise division permits separating madness from sanity" (Green, 1990, pp. 104–105). The use of the word "borderline" when it comes to differentiating mental pathology and mental health, then, is something of a misnomer, or at least gives rise to misunderstanding; it is not a line or division but a "vast territory", an expansive and perhaps overlapping realm reaching into each.

Edmond Jabès, who shared the same background in Egypt and destiny in France of being in-between, though as a poet not a psychoanalyst, wrote while still living in Cairo in the early 1940s, "Constamment en pays étranger, le poète se sert de la poésie comme interprète", which may be translated as: "Constantly in a foreign country, the poet makes use of poetry as his interpreter" (Jabès, 1959, p. 208). A perennial stranger, the poet is concerned with interpreting borders and what occurs inside and outside them, and of making their qualities visible. The interpretative drive—or is it rather the translational drive?—is part and parcel of a poet's self experience, a continuously transformative aesthetic ontology. If I were to substitute "psychoanalyst" for "poet" and "psychoanalysis" for "poetry" in Jabès's aphorism, I believe that we would come one step closer to sensing not only what characterises André Green's psychic condition but also the pertinence of his clinical thinking.

When we discuss a book with another person, such a dialogue can be thought of as object presenting, the paradigm being how the mother presents an object to her baby. In talking about an aesthetic object, there occurs a verbal and nonverbal exchange that reveals the way by which one subject relates to another. I recall how in 2006, in the courtyard behind the rue Saint-Jacques at the former premises of the Paris Psychoanalytic Society while waiting for his seminar to begin, André Green came up to me and asked what I was working on. It happens that I had just given a lecture on the painter Zoran Music in which I discussed Green's disobjectalising function—in which first one disqualifies the other so that the other may be eliminated—in relation to how Music, while in Dachau, managed to sketch his fellow prisoners. With his own means he objectalised (or re-objectalised) them through recording their experience in the face of death, imminent or realised.

This was a desperate and potentially life-threatening expression of the life drive when confronted with an absolute form of destructiveness (Jaron, 2008).

André Green told me that he wished to see the lecture notes and the conversation ended with a mutual smile as we walked together in silence up to the seminar room. Shortly afterwards, with some trepidation, I sent them to him. He wrote back and I was relieved when he gave them his approval. The work of Zoran Music, moreover, made him think of another painter who had survived the camps, Miklos Bokor, with whom, he indicated, he was well acquainted (Green, 1995 and 2011c). He then added that he had just finished a book on the death drive. He said, however, that he did not know if I would subscribe to the assertions set out in this new work, as I had, earlier, regarding *On Private Madness*. *On Private Madness* dealt largely with the borderline concept and the treatment of borderline states while the subject of *On the Destruction and Death Drives* was principally what its title suggested. While reading it and thinking about my own clinical work—to speak nothing of the dark passages of history, if only those in which Music and Bokor found themselves ensnared—the metapsychology of the death drive and the urge to destroy was, however, immediately made clear to me.

A few thoughts on terminology. The expression, *drive theory*, is a not-so literal translation of Freud's *Trieblehre*. While *Lehre* in English might connote "theory", it chiefly means "lesson" or "teaching". Furthermore, it is less doctrinal (though some may see it in this way) than forming part of a body of knowledge, one moreover susceptible to revision. Consistent with Freud, André Green employs *pulsion* throughout *Pourquoi les pulsions de destruction ou de mort?* (as in his other works) and my translation, *drive*, follows this usage. Yet this differs from how *Trieb* appears in the *Standard Edition* as *instinct*, a choice denounced by Lacan, for instance, in his 1964 seminar (Lacan, 1964, p. 49). And yet, explaining his decision to go for *instinct*, James Strachey argued that at mid-century the English language had no satisfactory equivalent for the German word. Opting for *drive* would require, he contended, "a very brave man seriously to argue that rendering Freud's '*Trieb*' by 'drive' clears up the situation" (Strachey, 1966, p. xxv). I presume, however, that one hundred years after the publication of *Beyond the Pleasure Principle* (1920), not only a specialised knowledge of Freud's essential terminology but likewise a broader one has been acquired, and so Strachey's decision has been reversed. If Strachey favoured *instinct*, perhaps this was in fact because it was what was acceptable—at least he thought it so—at the time (the appearance of the first English translation was nearly simultaneous with the publication of the German edition). The drive, specifically the death drive, was itself the source of discomfort consistent, as Green repeatedly shows, with the discomfort felt by those analysts for whom the very idea was inadmissible. For him, the refusal of the metapsychological concept of the death drive amounts to nothing less than a rejection of the *full* contribution of Freudian psychoanalysis to the understanding of human nature. Further, though perhaps less important yet still advisable, I have chosen "investment" for "cathexis", Strachey's rendering of *Besetzung*.

Revisions have been made not only to the *Standard Edition*'s translations of Freudian terminology but also to the titles of some of Freud's books and essays. *Moses and Monotheism* (1939) is given here as *The Man Moses and Monotheistic Religion*, and especially important to *On the Destruction and Death Drives, Discomfort in Culture* replaces *Civilization and Its Discontents* (1930). Laurence Kahn argues that translating the title of Freud's final work as *The Man Moses and Monotheistic Religion* is preferable in order to emphasise, following Freud, that Moses was a *man* (Kahn, 2022). My decision to render *Das Unbehagen in der Kultur* as *Discomfort in Culture* is motivated by the observation that the usual translation doesn't convey the meaning of the first term, so fundamental to Freud's thesis (stated in a word here but developed by Green in Section 3.1) that cultural processes impinge on the drives and thereby arouse frustration, with everything that such renunciation or compromise implies. According to Strachey, Freud himself suggested *Man's Discomfort in Civilization* to the book's initial translator, Joan Riviere, "but," he added, "it was she herself who found the ideal solution of the difficulty in the title that was finally adopted" (Strachey, 1961, p. 60). Other possibilities, however, include *disquiet* or *unease* or, as Strachey floated, *malaise* (in fact, retained for the French translations, *Le Malaise dans la culture* or *la civilisation*, depending on the translator). Be that as it may, the suggestion to give *das Unbehagen* as *discomfort* is, it seems to me, quite sufficiently accurate: one might think that *disquiet* is preferable because *discomfort* is both physical and psychical while the former word describes a categorically mental disturbance, that is, worry or unease. But in this specific work Freud discusses the impact of civilising processes on the drive, which he defined in "Instincts and their vicissitudes" (or, rather, "Drives and the drives' fate") as a "frontier concept between the mental and somatic, as the psychical representative of the stimuli originating from within the organism and reaching the mind, as a measure of the demand made upon the mind for work in consequence of its continuity with the body" (Freud, 1915, p. 122). To my mind, the *discomfort* associated with the fortunes of the drive helpfully combines what is both psychic and somatic and further implies their continuity (Freud speaks of *Zusammenhang*). Lastly, the English of the title, "Das Unheimliche" (1919) (Strachey's "The 'uncanny'", with the key term placed, as it were, in scare quotes), in which Freud displays his audacious yet fastidious genius as a rigorous philological psychoanalyst, is given as "The unhomely".

Like Freud's language use, I have tried to render Green's thinking, expressed with his characteristic combativeness, as clearly yet as faithfully as possible. At times, however, he uses words that are uncommon in French (e.g., *néantisation* and *psychisation*) and so, where needed, an occasional explanatory note has been added. Words or expressions such as *après-coup* or jouissance have not been commented on as they are more familiar to English-speaking analysts, though Rosine Jozef Perelberg (Perelberg, 2006) on the former and Darian Leader (Leader, 2021) on the latter can be consulted with profit as to their meaning. The French terms *intrication* and *désintrication* are translated as *intrication* and *disintrication*; while rare in English, they are nevertheless attested to and so cannot be translated as *fusion* (*fusion*) and *defusion* (*défusion*) or *binding* (*liaison*) and *unbinding* (*déliaison*), all of which moreover are frequently employed by different authors including Green himself in discussions on drive theory. Where Green regularly shortens titles of Freud's works (e.g., *Au-delà...* for *Beyond the Pleasure Principle*), full titles are restored. Quotations of passages from his own works have been translated especially for this volume. André Green chose Montaigne for the epigraph to this work, and I feel that Florio's translation, contemporary with Shakespeare though here somewhat modernised, is suitable for the English edition.

Warm thanks are due to the members of the Boston Group for Psychoanalytic Studies (BGPS) and, in particular, Howard B. Levine and

David G. Power, whose comments on a draft of this work I have greatly benefited from, and further to Ana de Staal of Ithaque Editions and Kate Pearce of Phoenix Publishing House.

References

Freud, S. (1915). Instincts and their vicissitudes. *S. E., 14*: 117–140. London: Hogarth.

Freud, S. (1919). The "uncanny". *S. E., 17*: 219–256. London: Hogarth.

Freud, S. (1920). *Beyond the Pleasure Principle. S. E., 18*: 7–64. London: Hogarth.

Freud, S. (1930). *Civilization and Its Discontents. S. E., 21*: 57–146. London: Hogarth.

Freud, S. (1939). *Moses and Monotheism. S. E., 23*: 6–137. London: Hogarth.

Green, A. (1986). *On Private Madness*. London: Hogarth.

Green, A. (1990). *La folie privée: psychanalytse des cas-limites* [*Private Madness: Psychoanlysis of Borderline Patients*]. Paris: Gallimard.

Green, A. (1993). *Le travail du négatif* [*The Work of the Negative*]. Paris: Minuit.

Green, A. (1995). Effacer les traces [Effacing the traces]. In: Miklos Bokor, *Le délire de l'homme* [*The Delirium of Man*] (pp. 25–27). Caen: Musée des Beaux-Arts.

Green, A. (1999). *The Work of the Negative*. A. Weller (Trans.). London: Free Association.

Green, A. (2010). *Illusions et désillusions du travail psychanalytique* [*Illusions and Disillusions of Psychoanalytic Work*]. F. Urribarri (Pref.). Paris: Odile Jacob.

Green, A. (2011a). *Illusions and Disillusions of Psychoanalytic Work*. A. Weller (Trans.). London and New York: Routledge.

Green, A. (2011b). Les cas-limites: de la folie privée aux pulsions de destruction et de mort [Borderline cases: From private madness to the destruction and death drives]. *Revue française de psychanalyse, 75*(2): 375–390.

Green, A. (2011c). L'homme exilé [Exiled man]. In: A. Becker & A. Bernou (Eds.), *Cahier Miklos Bokor* [*Miklos Bokor Notebook*] (pp. 113–115). Périgueux: William Blake & Co./Paris: Institut National d'Histoire de l'Art.

Jabès, E. (1959). *Je bâtis ma demeure, poèmes 1943–1957* [*I Build My Dwelling, Poems 1943–1957*]. Gabriel Bounoure (Pref.). Paris: Gallimard.

Jaron, S. (2008). *Zoran Music: voir jusqu'au coeur des choses*. Paris: L'Echoppe. (The English language version, *Zoran Music: Seeing into the Life of Things*, may be found on https://fortnightlyreview.co.uk/2015/07/zoran-music/)

Kahn, L. (2022). The probable in Nazi times: The opposing fates of the mystical and the law. S. Jaron (Trans.). In: L. J. Brown (Ed.), *On Freud's "Moses and Monotheism"*. London and New York: Routledge.

Lacan, J. (1964). *Le séminaire, livre XI: les quatre concepts fondamentaux de la psychanalyse* [*Book XI of the Seminar: The Four Fundamental Concepts of Psychoanalysis*]. J.-A. Miller (Ed.). Paris: Le Seuil, 1973.

Leader, D. (2021). *Jouissance: Sexuality, Suffering and Satisfaction*. Cambridge: Polity.

Perelberg, R. J. (2006). The Controversial Discussions and *après-coup*. *International Journal of Psychoanalysis*, 87(5): 1199–1220, and erratum, 87(6): 1722.

Strachey, J. (1961). Editor's introduction. In: S. Freud, *Civilization and Its Discontents. S. E., 21*: 59–63. London: Hogarth.

Strachey, J. (1966). Notes on some technical terms whose translation calls for comment. In: S. Freud, *S. E., 1*: xxiii–xxvi. London: Hogarth.

On the edition of 2010

The first French edition of this book appeared in March 2007 and was published by Panama in its series "Cyclo". It went out of print shortly afterwards. We wish to thank Ithaque for taking on the second edition, which is enhanced by a bibliography and index. The 2007 edition included illustrations that could not be reproduced here. It was likewise necessary to do without extracts from the works referred to in the original appendix. What appears in the current edition is the complete text of the Panama edition, to which I have made a few corrections.

I am especially happy that this text continues to circulate which, whether rightly or wrongly, I consider as one of my most important works.

André Green, May 2010

In memory of
Évelyne

Although they say that, in virtue itself, the last scope of our aim is voluptuousness.

The end of our cariere is death. It is the necessary object of our aim ...

Had you not death, you would then incessantly curse and cry out against me that I had deprived you of it. I have of purpose and unwittingly blended some bitterness amongst it, that so seeing the commodity of its use, I might hinder you from over greedily embracing or indiscreetly calling for it. To continue in this moderation, that is neither to fly from life nor to run to death (which I require of you), I have tempered both the one and other between sweetness and sourness.

> —Montaigne, *Essays*, Book 1, Chapter XX,
> translated from the French by John Florio

Foreword

André Green

Is death truly the aim of a drive?[9] If we date the hypothesis of the death drive to 1920, it seems especially curious that references in the past hardly make it possible to credit any precursors and, after this date, not many successors. There are however a few exceptions. They include the remarkable breakthrough of Schopenhauer—without doubt the philosopher closest to Freud, as he himself acknowledged—and, in his wake, widening the breach opened by Schopenhauer if only better to close it up so as to give us the hope stripped away by him, Nietzsche, who appears as the most effective antidote against the pessimism of Freudian theory. The "preposterous death drive", remarked Deleuze.

Moving farther back into the past, if the patronage of Empedocles is invoked by Freud himself, this pre-Socratic philosopher remains quite isolated. None among the materialists of Antiquity comes to Freud's rescue. In philosophy, the harvest is thus poor, and its more recent developments, only confirm the trend.

---

[9] I wish to thank Litza Guttieres-Green and Hélène Boulais for putting the finishing touches to the manuscript.

And so, we must abandon any hope for philosophy. In that case should we fall back on the psychoanalysts themselves? Alas, such a solution is hardly viable. For either they—the finest—are counted among the fiercest critics of the "death drive"; or they embraced the concept without shoring up their support with well-argued analysis; or, lastly, they distorted its signification with an eye to simplifying it, though without however truly helping us to understand what it was about.

Should we call on those with common sense as backup? Certainly not, for there is nothing more alien to common sense than an understanding of psychoanalytic theory, above all when it comes to the death drive. There remains but the illusion of the support of those whom we had not dared summon to the discussion due to a rightful doubt, of those "enamoured with lucidity". For each conceives lucidity in his or her own way, all the while taxing the opinions of others with obscurantism.

Living with the idea of bearing a death-force fundamentally directed at oneself is hardly easy to admit. It is less so, in any case, than the idea that we are all murderers, that we are ever ready to plead legitimate defence or the need to survive so as to strike out at another.

Let's take a side: psychoanalytic thought repels those who try to assimilate it from the outside in so far as its fundamental postulates and theorems are at odds with ordinary thinking. If the power of the conviction of ideas is often defeated in this matter, at the very least "time for reflection"[10] can be of help so as to nurture the questions and answers in light of the thinking accorded in this book to experience.

A remark before moving on. I have sided with Freud's ideas on the death drive if only to suggest a slightly different version of it, and so it has been for a very long time. However, it was while writing this work that I first understood something in particular about the questions that the death drive raise. But in truth I should say that the answers I offer are based as much on my ideas as on the reflections of a good many post-Freudian authors who have influenced me. For all that, I am under no illusion that I have brought this to a completion but have merely taken it up a notch.

Croagnes, Summer 2006

---

[10] The title of a defunct journal edited by J.-B. Pontalis.

CHAPTER 1

Foundations

1.1 Hypotheses on the genesis of the death drive

We ought not shy away from contending with Freud's most speculative metapsychology, that which at times roils us due to its impression of being inimical to retreating from the paradise of ideas while nevertheless legislating on problems that concern our clinical practice at its deepest, for example, when it elevates itself to examining notions as prevalent and fundamental as life and love, as destructiveness and death.

In his very last theorising on these questions, Freud drops his final hypothesis dealing with the enigma of the repetition compulsion. The repetition compulsion and the beyond of the pleasure principle fall under an unexpected, novel explanation: that of the drive as restoration of a prior state. Yet a hypothesis with so broad a scope must be judged in light of its ramifications. In order to validate such an idea, it needs to be combined with a theory of beginnings, its precondition. At this point Freud experiences some embarrassment. Up till then, the drive had served as guarantee for the primal, above all when its primitive aim was pleasure, when theory, all the while accepting the existence of fundamental drive conflicts, only conceptualised them in the *as-yet defined* frame of the life drives whose classification and definition had thus far not appeared. It is therefore incorrect to assert that the life drives already existed, but it is still necessary to highlight that nothing of what will be sorted with death provided or had at its disposal a drive support which had not yet been conceived. Nor could anything, even hypothetically, be inscribed in the frame of the life drives—because such a concept did not yet exist. All manifestations related to aggressiveness still belonged to the inner vicissitudes of the sexual libido, a thesis that Adler had advanced in his own way earlier during psychoanalysis's beginnings and which Freud wanted nothing of, at least in this guise. In brief, death was but the exhaustion of life's, and thus the libido's, potential—just as, moreover, many contemporary psychoanalysts continue to think.

The hypothesis of the death drive shakes all of this up. If the return to a prior state of life becomes the blanket aim of any drive, out of what the final or initial prior state might be constituted had to be clarified.

As always with Freud, the introduction of a new concept puts the equilibrium of the whole into question and necessitates another conceptualising than that which had prevailed till then. No attempt at understanding the impact of the death drive can do without attentively reflecting on the opposite group and which saw the birth of other ideas in place of earlier concepts which till then were quite solidly established, even if later additions would modify their signification. This can be said of the theoretical phase opposing narcissistic libido and object libido, which in my opinion merits being called the second drive theory, thereby reserving for the understanding of 1920 the denomination of the *third* and final drive theory. But fate has decided otherwise and sees in the 1913–1914 stage merely an incident which misdirected Freud's judgement—by his own admission. He reproached himself at the time for having been influenced unbeknownst to him, and even against his wishes, by a disciple who afterwards became his adversary (C. G. Jung). Convention decided to keep the expression, the second and final drive theory, for the ideas spelled out solely in 1920. It nevertheless remains to be understood in what way the reshaping of 1914 paved the way for the revolution of 1920.

One novelty of the understanding of 1920 is to present itself as having two dimensions, synchronic and diachronic. On the one hand, as with his earlier concepts, it offers a new synchronic image of the psyche's constitution. This is what impels Freud to maintain that the life drive and death drive coexist from birth. But alongside and doubtless beyond this, the rationalisation for the death drive must be associated with a *phylogenetic* and thus diachronic perspective which, to that end, in theory unwaveringly returns to the beginnings of life.

This point of view is not expressed in the final drive theory in isolation, contrary to earlier assertions. Such is the surprise that must have awaited readers of *Beyond the Pleasure Principle*. They hardly suspected that the questioning of the pleasure principle should be accompanied by a reflection on the beginnings of life in order to account for the diverse organisations of the psyche. This is a position which most certainly takes up some of the assertions of "Project for a scientific psychology" (1950) of 1895 but which were without precedent in Freud's published work.[11] I admit that I have often been irritated by the speculation of 1920, not resolving to accept it as a sort of playful exercise, a fanciful digression of the mind which grants itself some imaginative licence in the midst of often arid thinking. But even Freud's most daring speculations, to speak nothing of the most gratuitous, are accompanied by a reflection which returns the analyst to problems which, notwithstanding, are widely familiar.

The fact remains that the synchronic perspective isn't exactly lacking in purpose. The synonymic terms that Freud suggested as corollaries of his invention attest to this: *life* drives–*death* drives and *love* drives–*destruction* (or *aggression*) drives, all of which may be subsumed behind a pair which is more theoretical-clinical than speculative, specifically, binding–unbinding. Each different formulation consists in nuances that Freud naturally enlarges on. This habit isn't entirely new. How in effect could he assert that the narcissistic libido/object libido distinction bore no relationship to the most recent ideas? Was it forgotten that before theorising narcissism, Freud very early on gave a name to the "narcissistic neuroses" which at the time encompassed the psychoses in general? He then had to reserve this denomination for manic-depressive psychosis, whereas the earlier "narcissistic neuroses" would bear the name of

---

[11] "Project for a scientific psychology" was published, contrary to Freud's wish, only after the belated discovery of its manuscript.

psychoses, the destructiveness that they contain henceforth serving to characterise them.

The proof that the new positions are accompanied by a reintegrating aim may be distinguished among his most abstract speculations. Thus the return to the erstwhile problem of sadism, which contains more ambiguities than Freud had previously imagined. It isn't so much about Adler that we think, but the inner development of Freud's thinking dominated first and foremost by the libido alone and including anal-sadistic regression. He henceforth sets about formulating a new dialectic relating death (destruction, sadism) to the libido (narcissistic first, then object). In 1920 Freud argues that he had always recognised a sadistic component of the sexual drive. Notwithstanding, he now envisages, above and beyond the possibility that this might build itself up into perversion, that it might free itself from this combination (disintrication–reintrication). Thus unbinding is possible, but this isn't what Freud wants to emphasise; rather, it is the gradual transition which permits relegating sadism to a secondary position. He then formulates the hypothesis of the pushing-back of sadism under the influence of the narcissistic drive: "Is it not plausible to suppose that this sadism is in fact a death drive which, under the influence of the narcissistic libido, has been forced away from the ego and has consequently only emerged in relation to the object?" (Freud, 1920, p. 54). Only later is sadism's destructive aim, which seeks the ego's annihilation, uncovered. Sadism subsequently manifests itself in an amorous ascendancy through the desire to dominate the object.

Let's have a look at Freud's rhetoric. He begins with a familiar clinical phenomenon, even if it has given rise to diverse, if not divergent, theorising. This gives birth to the hypothesis of associating sadism with the death drive through gaining purchase on the intrications and disintrications of the sexual drive, a "vicissitude" of the sadistic component of the libido in its perverse form and its new goal, destruction, in the new perspective. Now this goal is in fact dictated by the diachronic perspective: the sadism of the sexual drive is *cast out* from the psyche by the development of the narcissistic libido. The problem of following the developments of the non-destructive sadistic libido leads to bringing out the initial effects of what is known as the life drive, which is put in service of ego defence. Thus narcissistic power, endeavouring to make life triumph, strives in its initial phases to impede the ego from sinking into destruction, for lack of which no psychic structuring would be possible. This step anticipates that of 1925 in which the analysis of the mechanism of negation results in a two-fold outcome: first, the repelling of the foreign(er), the bad, and the hated outside and, simultaneously, the constitution of a purified pleasure-ego.

Narcissism is thus the principal victor in the conflict of the life drive–death drive battle of the behemoths *to the advantage of the life drives*. This step hypothesises the counter-offensive of the death drive, which seeks to annul the imbalance introduced by the life drive. Thus, historically, we have turned away from a narcissism initially conceived on a death-yielding mode (the psychoses) to an integrating life narcissism, which gives ground for my theory of *two* narcissisms, life and death narcissism.[12]

In sum, we see Freud trying to make his final theory of the drives, which in a way seems to implicate their simultaneity and their concomitance, compatible with a new approach which seeks to shed light on the succession of death drives (seeking the return to a prior, pre-vital state) and the drives of the erotic libido (a more recent manifestation), narcissism playing the fundamental role of a step in which is made manifest the first predominance of Eros. We should recall that the ego can only construct itself on a design of "purified" pleasure. Freud doesn't specify what this consists of, but we understand that it must momentarily purify itself of the temptation of destructiveness, whose aim is a return to non-life.

At this point, we thus observe the need to formulate what is first and then what comes next, and to search for the mode by which the transition from one to the other may be affected. The previous theorising (self-preservation drives and sexual drives, narcissistic libido and object libido) was restricted to formulating a non-unified coexistence and founded itself on a deep theoretical-clinical intuition. In 1920, all the while basing himself on a very solid structural foundation, Freud's final drive theory adds a dimension absent from the earlier approaches founded on phylogenesis.

We shall examine in greater detail the two notions—the diachronic and the synchronic—in relation to the idea of the death drive. The first,

---

[12] Translator's note: Green is referring to his work, *Life Narcissism, Death Narcissism* (first published in 1983 and then in English in 2001). See also Section 1.3.

that which Freud is in agreement with, is to imagine how original (organic) matter unendowed with life is moved by means of an active force as yet totally unrepresentable, that is, scarcely capable of bearing the denomination of life drive, without any further specification. What is important is that which follows this event: the tension revealed at the time in the substance in the process of "vitalisation" is threatened by a recurrence aiming at levelling it again, that is, annulling this tension, neutralising it[13] *in order to reinstate a prior state* of *non-life*, that is, of non-tension. Thus is born, according to Freud, the first drive: "the first drive came into being: the drive to return to the lifeless state" (Freud, 1920, p. 38). In other words, the first drive may only be a death drive. In brief, the *primal* drive is the death drive. This vision depends, we should recall, on the phylogenetic hypothesis.

The other basic hypothesis, which is non chronological, posits a vision of simultaneity; death drives and life drives coexist from the beginning—we should no doubt add, "in the individual". We observe that the first angle is speculative and prehistoric and the second is conceptual and based on the balance of the theory in ontogenesis, abandoning prehistory to speculation and making the entire load weigh on the interpretation of clinical practice.

Freud feels his way along: "We started out from the great opposition between the life and death drives. Now object-love itself presents us with a second example of a similar polarity—that between love (or affection) and hate (or aggressiveness)" (Freud, 1920, p. 53). Freud hypothetically constructs the relationship between these two orders of givens and wishes to pinpoint a link, making it possible to go from one to the other. It is thus that here again he gives priority to the diachronic dimension, even when considering the ontogenetic angle.

And this is where narcissism comes to the rescue. Our ambition has been to detail the thinking underlying this development since, to our knowledge, Freud gives no account of it. Freud's aim is to consider narcissism as the primary link between the death drive and life drive. That said, if we take a step back, we find that Freud's coherence is remarkable. It is nevertheless an approach marked by obstinacy.

---

[13] "endeavoured to cancel itself out" (Freud, 1920, p. 38) recalls the French translation *annuler, éliminer, neutraliser* [to annul, to eliminate, to neutralise], which, in our view, differs from *niveler* [to level] as too elliptic.

First, there is vagueness such that nothing may be differentiated (chaos?). Then come the first identifiable investments (libido attached to the subject's body, bodily eroticism—the "auto-" period—by primary unification, and so on). This is followed by the constitution of the stage of primary unification: narcissism properly speaking, autoeroticism which opposes itself to the disappearance of what's been gained but which cannot withstand time as such. An intervention which affects the investment and the constitution of the object follows it. The effect of this investment is not only to bring the object into play, but to compel the psychic structure to deploy itself and show what it hides within its folds, disclosing its priorities and ultimate aim.

Freud describes all of this as occurring in two phases. His initial statement concerns the insufficiency of life in organic matter, which at bottom isn't much different from the accounts of contemporary biology.[14] The second way of putting it eliminates the temptation of going back in time in relation to the disequilibrium of life, even though no equivalent in science touches on it other than what one calls the return of catastrophism, which nevertheless is part and parcel of the twists and turns of life. New conceptualising however does go into it.[15] Lastly, the clinically appreciable step in the theories of narcissism makes it possible to consider the ego's beginnings and their vicissitudes in its relation to the object.

1.2 From the repetition compulsion (constraint)[16] to primal reproduction

Narcissism is the cornerstone in the construction of the death drive. From 1914 on, Freud unfailingly refers to it among the problems that he is led to handle. In *Beyond the Pleasure Principle*, its role is still capital,

---

[14] Cf. Michel Cassé, "Le cosmos, conceptions et hypothèses" [The Cosmos, Concepts and Hypotheses], in Morin (Ed.) (1999, pp. 26–32), as well as the contributions of Auguste Commeyras, Sébastien Balibar, and Jean-Marc Lévy-Leblond in the same volume.

[15] Cf. Jean Claude Ameisen's theories on cell suicide in the Appendix.

[16] This is the usual English translation given for "repetition compulsion". The French edition of Freud's complete works nonetheless opts for "repetition constraint" (*contrainte de répétition*). Both are defensible, but the advantage of *compulsion* is that it emphasises its kinship with *drive* (*pulsion*), even if *Zwang* highlights the relationship to *constraint*.

but this might already be the beginning of a waning, and, in subsequent theorising, it becomes decreasingly present. Several years would go by between "Remembering, repeating and working-through" and *Beyond the Pleasure Principle*.

But let's linger for a moment with "Remembering, repeating and working-through". Might we be tempted to accuse Freud of skewing the facts and coming up with only what he was looking for? A close, attentive reading of the text disproves this completely. Considering the discovery of repetition, initially Freud doesn't in the least consider the death drive. He simply discloses a form of unexpected resistance. He's far from rushing to a conclusion. At the end of the essay, driven by a frankly optimistic attitude, he advises the analyst to observe carefully, to study this particular form of resistance and to take—simultaneously suggesting this to the analysand—whatever time may be required in order to work-through this new cause for the analysis's stagnation. It's clear that Freud doesn't initially observe any insurmountable obstacle in it. In all likelihood, many years will need to go by before he realises that he is dealing with something entirely different from what he had first anticipated. This is perhaps why he grants himself six years before coming to the pessimistic conclusion that it is a matter of an effect of the death drive. There is thus no preconception or begging the question.

One may even think that Freud himself takes time over pondering it. But nothing suggests this throughout a study of the texts published between 1914 and 1920. During this period, however, one sees a pulling-together of the theory at its highest level with the "Papers on meta-psychology" of 1915 and a recapitulation of what is essential, for the non-specialist reader, with the *Introductory Lectures on Psychoanalysis*. Nothing heralds the ideas of *Beyond the Pleasure Principle* until 1920. This is thus a breakthrough due to a reordering of the guiding concepts; in brief, a "narcissistic" movement which attributes a novel unity to the pre-existing elements of the theory.

I'm inclined to bring the influential role of two events into play. First, the widespread slaughter of the First World War, the inexhaustible source of meditations which triggered two very interesting essays by Freud[17] but in which one seeks in vain an allusion to the death drive.

---

[17] "Thoughts for the times on war and death: 1/ The Disillusionment of the war; 2/ Our attitude towards death" (1915).

The second, which is nearly contemporary, concerns the clinical thinking shaken up by the analysis of the Wolf Man.

The "Papers on metapsychology" likewise close in 1915 with "Mourning and melancholia", whose initial hypotheses will be the object, in 1923, of a reinterpretation more directly related to the death drive. Moreover, after *Beyond the Pleasure Principle*, he expresses his conviction with increasing frequency that humans bear within themselves an element of hatred as well as a penchant for aggression and destruction, and thus for cruelty.

And so a reflection on culture and a revaluation of clinical practice, leaving him ever more distraught, go hand-in-hand in Freud's thinking. These questions call for such radical answers that Freud seems from the beginning to dread affirming them with excessive certainty, as if they were likely to alienate any number of his disciples. He first expresses his thoughts while minimising their import by granting to them the status of a personal preference which no one should feel obliged to share, in order to then edge towards the assertion of a certitude which nothing could put into doubt.

Perhaps so as to steer clear of rejection and incomprehension, Freud refuses to open his eyes in the analysis of the Wolf Man (between 1910 and 1912 and first written up from March to May 1914). The case doubtless troubled him to the point of blinding his judgement; all the more that, centred on the primal scene and keen to get the better of Jung, he in all likelihood underestimated the impact of the other discoveries which took him by surprise. As if he could not believe his eyes, he was constrained to deny what the Russian, an expert in repetition compulsion, had taught him once more. Sergei Pankejeff subsequently had the opportunity of providing a great many examples of this to analysts who succeeded Freud. They took no notice of it. And so it was until his death. The particularity of his clinical structure eluded Freud himself, who misunderstood that it illustrated a kind of masochistic organisation reflecting a form of negative therapeutic reaction. Freud could have examined from this moment the part that could be played in this vicissitude which he was in the process of working out as the death drive. But chance diverted the blows destined for the patient and it was his wife—the unfortunate Theresa, about whom Freud was likewise greatly mistaken—who killed herself without warning or drawing the least attention to the ties with Freud's analysand's pathology.

The writing of *Beyond the Pleasure Principle* is moreover contemporary with that of "The unhomely" (1919) in which, after 1914, Freud first alludes to the death drive. One cannot imagine two writings more dissimilar than the latter, in which its material is largely drawn from language and literature and which leans heavily on narcissism, and the former, which plunges us into the mystery of the origins of life and moves forward by way of speculations, yet in which one finds only a single, understated allusion to narcissism. These novel ideas give the impression of an intent to move mountains, stir up oceans, and shake the depths of the psyche's foundations. They abandon any recourse to the idea of representation to the very point of renouncing giving us a like image which could replace it. In vain, *Beyond the Pleasure Principle* attests to the disillusion concerning the belief in pleasure as a guide to life and the construction of the psychic world. Rebecca would have to remove her gown[18] once again but, this time around, Freud goes straight to the point, to the drive world as it is and not to the "representatives" making it possible to represent it itself.

Pointing out these contradictory attitudes or underscoring their coincidences, indicators of genuine discomfort during these years, would be sufficient enough. What above all holds our attention is Freud's radical will not to settle for treating these problems in a more or less superficial way through a partial theoretical reformation. This is surely because any solution of this kind would not satisfy him. In fact, what he then aspired to was a reworking touching on the foundations of the theory, the sole acceptable solution in Freud's eyes as time went by. And yet these ideas with their very great scope do not seem capable of resolving the technical problems facing Freud. This is why he seems to prefer creating a diversion and delay the time when he'll feel that he is in a position at once to modify the theory in accordance with the new direction that he wishes to give it and to make a reply to clinical problems. And so he'll have to wait till 1923 with *The Ego and the Id* in order to obtain a comprehensive perspective of the new metapsychology, which leads to the development of the structural model.

---

[18] An allusion to Freud's abandonment of the seduction theory in the popular and humorous form that he adopted: "Rebecca, take off your gown; you are no longer a bride" (Freud, 1897, p. 266).

Referring to the repetition compulsion in "The unhomely" and its absence in the analysis of the Wolf Man leads me to consider a two-fold piece of information. The first is that Freud has in no way "forgotten" this breakthrough, which resurfaces in one of his texts. The second is that its omission in a detailed case study seems to imply a certain reticence at revealing it too openly before it can be included in an articulated whole, which we find in *The Ego and the Id*. Still another period will have to come to pass in order to observe the culmination of his ideas with "The economic problem of masochism", in which we see him determined to affirm his hypotheses no matter the price to pay. The year 1924 is that which coincides with Freud's resolution to assert his ideas and the first thoroughgoing reappraisal of psychoanalytic technique (Ferenczi & Rank, 1924).

Discussion is henceforth open. Are the unsatisfactory results of analysis due to technique and Freud's theory or rather to what he himself refers to somewhat later as the role of impediments to healing in which is underscored the deleterious influence of the death drive, brazenly taken to task and held responsible? We know how much analysts will make use of the idea that the injunction to indict the death drive clears them of their faults and limits relatively unscathed. In my view, they have scarcely succeeded in demonstrating that they have anything better to offer.

And surely this is where we ought to try to search for the enigma of the resistance that the recourse to the death drive, one of the axioms of drive life according to Freud, gives rise to. What is at once its strength and weakness is that this thinking aspires to be both *physis and psyche, aletheia and origin, movement and cause of the movement, generator and product of the generation, and that it may only be understood as such*. This is too visionary for medical doctors and physiologists and too impure for philosophers; it is at once flesh and intellect, I and *Mind*.[19] And one must accommodate all these contradictions by rediscovering them through listening to the patient and reading the work of colleagues.

---

[19] Translator's note: In this formulation, Green juxtaposes French (*Je* for "I") and Greek (*Nous* for "mind").

One could say that enough is enough and that the era of overarching systems is done and gone. May we accept making do with only Being, Language, or Relation? No, we cannot, because not one of these terms means anything outside its relationship with the others, and perhaps also because we have missed something.

For what needs to be emphasised is that Freud does not add one more system to the pre-existing series but creates another system based on what the preceding ones could not encompass. Due to these objects defined by their very exclusion, Freud appropriates these so-called obscurities in order to take a stance unlike any other. Nor, then, does this amount to an anti-system standpoint, a path of least resistance that he denies himself, but rather a system which interests those which the others set aside, winding up sooner or later by leading to deadlocks. Perhaps even those which for Freud were gates allowing access to the theoretical-clinical solution that he had so much difficulty finding.

This is why *Beyond the Pleasure Principle* stands out as a productive period about which, with the benefit of hindsight, one must understand the composition, investigate the internal equilibrium, and seek out the supporting axes all the while remaining sensitive to their hybrid combination, and further ask the question—this naturally belongs to the death drive—concerning the risk of theoretical breakdown and being incapable of imagining what might lay claim to its replacement. *Beyond the Pleasure Principle* is a standby solution, for which *The Ego and the Id* will be the culmination—*Beyond the Pleasure Principle* being the *avant-coup* viewed *après-coup*. So here, then, we are driven by thinking, almost always afterwards discovering the meaning, function, and necessity of what it had posited earlier. Its "current overtaking" obliges us to retreat to the limits of an artificial realism which embroils more than unshackles us since the soil it is constructed on is too soft.

Is such thinking, which burrows while moving forward or moves forward while doing the spadework, entirely unprecedented? No. But what we find surprising is that we do not reach the endpoint of this question by examining the contents of what immediately precedes it. We've seen that the death drive is foreshadowed by next to nothing. And so? Is this a speculation without a source? It is rather a reunion with forgotten beginnings, but which now appears in a different light in order to herald a conclusion too often met with refusal.

As a matter of fact, the postulate to which Freud was forever faithful and which no less needed questioning implicitly encompasses death in its discourse and buries its head in the sand in the name of a peace for the soul which exists only as wishful thinking. Freud's friendship for Wilhelm Fliess, in the face of his obvious resistance, perhaps obliged the inventor of psychoanalysis to settle for less disconcerting formulas than those of "the Project for a scientific psychology". He remains silently faithful to it for close to forty years (from 1895 to 1935). This is why we need to go back to it.

"The Project for a scientific psychology" opens with hypotheses which give primacy of place to the idea that the psychic processes are quantitatively determined. The Q quantity (external quantity) finds itself subject to the general laws of movement. A fundamental principle concerns the activity of the psyche's components, a principle which, in Freud's words,

> promised to be highly enlightening since it appeared to comprise the entire function. This is the principle of neuronal inertia: that neurones tend to divest themselves of Q. On this basis, the structure and development as well as the functions [of neurons] are to be understood.
>
> (Freud, 1950, p. 296)

The process of discharge constitutes the primary function of the neuronal system. This functioning is, however, incompatible with the requirements of life which demand, in certain cases, a retention necessary for functioning: hunger, breathing, and sexuality, for instance. "In consequence, the neuronal system is obliged to abandon its original trend of inertia (that is, to bringing the level [of Qn] to zero). It must put up with [maintaining] a store of Qn sufficient to meet the demand for a specific action" (Freud, 1950, p. 297). Whence the "*endeavour at least to keep the* Qn *as low as possible*" (Freud, 1950, p. 297; emphasis added to the original) without eliminating it. This is *the effect of the principle of constancy*, a secondary function imposed by the requirements of life.

Ideally, if this were possible, the "inner needs" would aspire to a complete discharge analogous to the flight into the primary function. But this isn't the case and the ideal will have to settle, for lack of inertia which will make the system unexcitable, for a constancy which steers clear of the drawbacks of variations of grand amplitude.[20]

Put into more familiar terms, neuronal activity consists of two systems in compliance with two principles. The first, subject to the primary function, possesses the capacity to discharge itself in its entirety, as the operation of the central nervous system's relational activity suggests. This function comes into play each time that psychic activity finds itself confronted with the necessity of discarding what was called nociceptive excitations, presumed to bring the system into a state of unexcitability bringing about rest. But another system accompanies the preceding one: the system called autonomic (vegetative), which doesn't obey the same principle since it doesn't have the property of fully discharging itself of unpleasurable excitations. As this system depends most often on the other in order to calm the excitation which puts it into a state of unpleasure and because the action of the other can't be immediate, for a certain duration it must at the very least tolerate the tension, even when it is disagreeable. In contradistinction with the preceding system, it is governed by the secondary system, which makes indispensable tolerating a certain state of tension before it may be discharged by means of the specific action affected by the other. It is striking to observe an analogy with the ideas of Gerald Edelman,[21] who in our time opposes the non-self system and the self system (to which are connected values). A major issue is raised here, that is, the postulate of similarity between death and rest; and how what was the legitimate quest of rest becomes a yearning for death. Is it in order to find rest or to kill the noise of life that the death drive is called in?

Freud next keeps up, following the discovery of psychoanalysis, a lengthy discussion on the relationship between the principle of constancy and the principle of inertia. But what he remains attached to is that activity having as its goal the suppression of the inner tension produced by stimuli. Whence, later on, the renewal in interest in Barbara Low and her *principle of Nirvana*, which returns to the theme

---

[20] See our detailed consideration of the question in Green (1983). The interested reader may turn to pages 84 to 89 in the French edition.
[21] Cf. Edelman (1992 and 2004) as well as Edelman and Tononi, *A Universe of Consciousness: How Matter Becomes Imagination* (2000).

of Freud's early principle of inertia and likewise aims at the abolition of all tension. This is what Freud revisits in *Beyond the Pleasure Principle* while this time around explicitly pushing for the abolition of tensions to the point of death, whereas the union of the life processes increases the level of these tensions whose synthesis it must achieve (see the end of Chapter 6 of *Beyond the Pleasure Principle*). The way is thus paved which postulates, in 1920, the existence of the death drives. But for Freud, the death drive is the *initial drive*, that which seeks to annul tensions born of the introduction of life into inert matter. The union of two cells tied together by "life", that is, reproduction, remains the model and will have as its outcome the idea of the life drive, sexuality insufficiently giving a reply to his questioning.[22]

In short, the necessity of binding precedes the search for pleasure. If the drive is always supposed to re-establish a prior state, what are we to think of the most primal state of life which has not been annihilated by the return to a state of non-life? Freud affected the shift from the notion of repetition to a term thought of as its equivalent, specifically, reproduction. So Freud's reflection brought him to consider a phenomenon which could have no guarantor in an individual's psychic life. The clinical dimension finds itself abandoned to the benefit of a biological speculation without any substratum in what we call mental life. Perhaps myth (Plato) informs us in this connection better than reflection because it authorises itself to delve into that which philosophical thinking eschews. Should we relate it to the bias of an eloquent fiction or is it rather rationality itself which conceals the prohibitions of thinking in its pleats because it hasn't yet discovered the intellectual tools to speak about them conceptually? Would this be a matter of a special case of figurability (Botella & Botella 2001)?

But is it so incontestable that our yearning for rest is pushed to such extremes? Admittedly, from its beginnings psychoanalysis has encountered these attitudes. And, with hindsight, what then is repression if not this very thing?[23]

---

[22] Freud compares Platonic myth with the Upanishads and its Babylonian equivalents.
[23] Cordelia Schmidt-Hellerau sees in "Lethe" (the river of forgetting) the metaphor for the death drive. We cannot subscribe to this hypothesis which tends towards a confusion, in our view, between repression and the destruction drive. Cf. Schmidt-Hellerau (2000).

So just as Hamlet ponders, "To Sleep, perchance to dream", we shall recite along with him, "To repress", but how might we face the return of the repressed since who can foresee what it will be, and how will we be armed in order to face up to it? What war will see the return of this peace so dearly obtained, and who can affirm that we'll inevitably emerge as victors? We doubtless have at our disposal a great storehouse of rationalisations, which are scarcely of any use.

Repetition has become the repetition of a model, that of the primordial epoch of life's origins. Henceforth, the reflection bears on the relationships between binding and unbinding, less debatable concepts, and on the reasons for the impossible return to death. Just as there can be no clinical practice without metapsychology, there can be no metapsychology without locating what entirely eludes psychology's grasp. Anything remotely approaching direct observation has nothing to say about it. Nothing is more difficult than observing these principles because the experience of transference, the very foundation of clinical thinking, difficultly withstands the seduction of a perceptible phenomenon, leaving out that it first needed to be conceived in order for it to be conceivable and discernible.

Sexuality and death are the two inventions of the species. Freud doesn't make this claim; rather, François Jacob does. So the step to take for psychoanalytic theory is to make a shift from sexuality to Eros (the life or love drives) and from death to the death drive.

We know that psychosexuality is the purview of psychoanalysis. But what does this "psycho" consist in, the "psycho" which designates the object of psychoanalysis? Put differently, how does the sexuality of the biologist adopt the characteristics which make it psychosexuality, that is, human sexuality? As to death, till then in psychoanalysis nothing had suggested that it was dedicated to raising the same issue. Freud left it to philosophy to tackle death, but lo and behold he changes his mind and returns to what he believes is his charge when he speculates on the death drive. And if one is absolutely defiant about it, it is advisable to submit for consideration what death in life is about.

In such a case, since we have placed our bets on myth as a fiction of what is unthinkable by reason alone, we ought to educe from Freud's writings the myth that helps us think the unthinkable, even if it subsequently means dismantling it in the hope of viewing it with greater clarity.

1.3 The retractable scaffolding of narcissism

In an earlier work, *Life Narcissism, Death Narcissism*, we stressed narcissism's singularity when it comes to theory. The part it plays ranges from an untheorised idea to its full theorising in 1915, and afterwards to its disappearance with only intermittent references to it occurring after 1920.

The explanation for this eclipse surely lies in the fact that, for Freud, the final drive theory relativised interest in the concept of narcissism suspected of drive monism. With the final drive theory, dualism's position makes a comeback and, after 1920, narcissism appears only occasionally without explicitly indicating the precise position it takes. Implicitly present from the beginnings of psychoanalysis, it is used in order to qualify certain forms of neuroses solely defined by their unanalysability due to the non-transferential quality of their supposedly fixed (stagnant) libido onto the ego (what are known as narcissistic neuroses). This is doubtless fully developed after the account of the Schreber case and for a period becomes a theoretical tool of the utmost importance. The addition of the final drive theory could hardly make it possible to broaden its theoretical status since to a great extent it again makes use of the drive dualism to which Freud remains especially attached, whereas for a time he had distanced himself from it. Narcissism had few excuses for being modified and retained since Freud specifically accused himself of taking interest in a monist point of view, which at the time when he was separating himself from Jung would only cast onto the theory the shadow of the dissident who had taken a position against the excessive role that Freud attributed to drive life. He was thus compelled to choose between having to give up narcissism and suggesting a change in theoretical status. The first solution—which was the one adopted—doesn't explain why, now and again, Freud returns to it without further pushing the reach and signification of its role in the new theory. As to the second stance, it didn't receive any consensus since neither Grünberger nor Kohut, despite making considerable advancements, really tried to solve the problem, namely: *What becomes of the theory of narcissism in relation to the concepts of the life drive and the death drive which succeed it?*

So it is that I suggested, in 1983, that we differentiate within Freud's late theory between *life narcissism*, which in general overlays itself on that described by Freud in 1914, and *death narcissism*. Whereas the first aspires to the ego's unity and executes an objectalising function, the second expresses the tendency to attain a zero degree of excitation in the service of a disobjectalising function, an activity in which the death drive predominates.

A final argument needs mentioning. Does the involvement of narcissism as an agent of unification not constitute an obstacle to gaining access to the repressed unconscious which, by definition, puts into question the ego's unity which tends to negate it? I preferred the solution of a Janus-faced narcissism. The first reason is that it in no way hinders the theoretical principle of a divided ego, even if part of it seeks unification, and willingly reflects an antagonism between life and non-life and even more radically pits a totalising form against a parcelling form, the result of fragmentation. For narcissism is bound, given its frailty, to the continuous threat of breaking up. This was implicit in the unifying narcissism of 1913 since Freud's elaborations were already underscoring its tendency to division (influence syndrome and observation delirium).[24] What was but a potentiality becomes, in my view, a constant temptation. As a threat, narcissism becomes in certain clinical forms the essential goal of an annihilating vocation[25] which we call, so as better to differentiate it from the preceding one, "negative narcissism", and which without a doubt constitutes one of the most devastating forms of the death drive.

Narcissism subsequently recedes after 1920. We have reached the point at which we believed that the recourse to myth alone could get us out of trouble. Of course, this myth was already at hand; all that needed to be done was to draw out the key elements of the text. It cannot be said that classical mythology has failed us. The myth of Sisyphus was a kind

---

[24] Translator's note: In French, influence syndrome ("I am forced to say" or "to act") and observation delirium ("I am being watched over") are clinical features of mental automation.

[25] Translator's note: In French, *vocation néantisante*. *Néantisant*, like the use of *néantisation* below, has no satisfactory equivalence in English. Possibly an echo of Sartre's *néantiser* ("to nihilate") and *néant* ("nothingness"), it implies a process of annihilating, voiding, or negating. Green uses the term likewise in Sections 2.2 and 2.5.

of illustration of the repetition compulsion and Aristophanes in Plato's *Symposium*, which Freud refers to in *Beyond the Pleasure Principle*, gave us a mythical narrative very similar to psychoanalytic thinking on sexual difference as related to the varieties of sexual choice.

Freud admitted that he was a mythologist ("drive theory is our mythology"). But he was at once an inventor of myths and an interpreter of their meaning. When he went into the most speculative content of his theories and saw himself incapable of continuing to use the language of science, which he however held as the only valid one, he allowed himself an incursion outside science in order to try and transmit what turned out as resistant to being expressed in scientific language.

> In the obscurity that reigns at present in drive theory, it would be unwise to reject any idea that promises to throw light on it. We started out from the great opposition between the life and death drives. Now object-love itself presents us with a second example of a similar polarity—that between love (or affection) and hate (or aggressiveness). If only we could succeed in relating these two polarities to each other and in deriving one from the other! From the very first we recognized the presence of a sadistic component in the sexual drive. As we know, it can make itself independent and can, in the form of a perversion, dominate an individual's entire sexual activity ... But how can the sadistic drive, whose aim it is to injure the object, be derived from Eros, the preserver of life? Is it not plausible to suppose that this sadism is in fact a death drive which, under the influence of the narcissistic libido, has been forced away from the ego and has consequently only emerged in relation to the object? It now enters the service of the sexual function. During the oral stage of organization of the libido, the act of obtaining erotic mastery over an object coincides with the object's destruction; later, the sadistic drive separates off, and finally, at the stage of genital primacy, it takes on, for the purposes of reproduction, the function of overpowering the sexual object to the extent necessary for carrying out the sexual act. It might indeed be said that the sadism which has been forced out of the ego has pointed the way

for the libidinal components of the sexual drive, and that these follow after it to the object. Wherever the original sadism has undergone no mitigation or fusion, we find the familiar ambivalence of love and hate in love life.

(Freud, 1920, pp. 53–54)

What impressive conceptual acrobatics! Examining it closely, we find:

1) *The postulates*: life and death drives; narcissistic libido, object libido—the stages of the latter and their goals.
2) *The principal movements*:
   a) Primary sadism (unintricated); death drive.
   b) Investment of the ego by the life drives: primary narcissism (investment and non-drive).
   c) Expulsion of primary sadism by the narcissistic libido; primary masochistic residue.
   d) Object narcissistic relay and development of the object libido:
      i) Oral stage; annihilation of the object (consumption);
      ii) Separation (without specification: anality?);
      iii) Stage of genital primacy; mastery of the sexual object;
      iv) Narcissistic expulsion, indicates the path towards the object to follow;
      v) Life drive-death drive intrication.
3) *The consequences of intrication*: love–hate ambivalence.

Regarding these figures of the myth which brings the protagonists together and pits them against each other, Freud describes the combinations of the narcissistic life or death drives and objectalisation. One point in particular retains our attention. It concerns the question asked by Freud as to how Eros, provisionally victor over death, may resist the movement arising from the prior return which would give its position back to the compulsion to die by harming the object. Take notice that Freud's construction obliges a return to the state of death—short of imagining a period during which Eros resists through opposing itself to its annihilation (*néantisation*). To the attempt at re-establishing the forces of death, Freud brings into conflict a vital, decisive counter-offensive. The forces which aspire to dispossessing life of its frail conquest, succumbing to the assaults of primary sadism, retreat under the effect of the mobilising of narcissistic libido which seeks to remain stable and refuses to recede. In evidence is Freud's skill in getting out of a tight corner. But if we consider the entirety of the passage, then we observe that during this period of time primary sadism *pre-empts* primary masochism. Freud has not yet adopted the idea that aggressiveness is but the consequence of the projected part of the death drive. The unprojected parts, those retained within the ego, constitute what is essential in the death drive, expressed in the form of masochism. This will later be at the root of endogenic death-work.

Freud considers that the aim of primary sadism is the damaging of the object. This is where we first find the destruction drive and the object brought together. I nevertheless believe that if Freud must make the narcissistic libido intercede at this point, it is because the object—and thus object libido—isn't yet identifiable as such. It only is in the form of a drive aspiring to indestructibility. Destructiveness first and foremost manifests itself against that which has managed to organise itself: the narcissistic libido which some today might call the self. In the end, if Freud draws attention to it, it's because it alone enjoys the beginnings of organisation. The object libido, while remaining in a state of aiming, cannot yet delineate the form of the object nor defend its autonomy nor define its mode of functioning. In other words, Freud postulates an *ontogenetic succession*: narcissistic libido, object libido. Narcissistic libido is older than object libido. Narcissism appears as the most central kernel of the life drives, as the supporting axis of any future edifice of the ego, the only one at the time capable of exerting an organised resistance vis-à-vis the death drives, and yet one must affirm that this central kernel is just as vulnerable.

There exists a sinister confirmation of this idea: before the Nazis had thought up the extermination camps, they nonetheless started to proceed with the destruction of the Jews by using artisanal methods. They did so by loading them into trucks and killing them with gas. At the very moment the Jews felt their lives threatened and in the grip of panic, they rushed towards the exit at the back, trampling anyone standing in the way and treading over those who had gone along with them and whom they most loved. There is no doubt that in the panic they lost any consciousness of how they reacted, which otherwise would have been tempered by their desire to spare their own. Be that as it may, the fact remains that the desire to save their own lives led them to ignore that they had become involuntary executioners of their children.

In appearance, the contradiction is an unsolvable yet necessary condition if we recall that the libido's narcissistic nature is responsible for it at the moment it is deprived of the supplement of object libido. This is consistent with Freud's ideas concerning narcissistic structures: they are autarkic and due to this are weakened by the absence of object libido, which only comes into play at a later time. As the foundation of the ego's organisation, it presents itself as especially frail in the event of libidinal loss. Think of the narcissistic neurosis par excellence, melancholia.

The quasi-exclusive investment is then that of the "libidinal supplement of the self-preservation drives".[26] So as to guarantee the survival of the life drive, resistance is organised around the libidinal supplement of the self-preservation drives. In short, the struggle for life is shored up by narcissism which is love and unity of self, itself emerging from the foundations of autoeroticism which maintains its acquisitions by attempting "to persevere in its being".[27]

Consequently, this investment may give rise to the compromise of a (narcissistic) body struggling against threatening death drives. *This might be what is found at the root of psychosomatic structures.* It is a complete, powerful, and vulnerable narcissism: the state of a bastion body, the refuge in which life is bivouacked and yet stricken by a weakness in object libido which might reinforce its fracture. A prodigious screen is established and appears unfailing, but if it cracks apart, the psychic structure is no more than a façade, an appearance, letting its frailty show through.

Freud comes to a radical conclusion: he must admit that the only true love is object-love. Self-love for the self's sake in narcissism is merely the refuge which, certainly, guarantees interim, partial, and temporary relief. But, as it happens, this occurs only in appearance. The psychic structure recognises the danger of the illusion and yet, from another point of view, it needs the illusion in order to help maintain it

---

[26] Freud's definition of narcissism.
[27] Some today insist on the role of the object in this transformation. Such an argument changes nothing, in our view, concerning Freud's construct.

at a sufficient level of activity and nourish self-esteem. It is a matter of *a purified narcissistic ego, but also a most vulnerable ego.*

This is narcissism as self-love brought to bear in the event of a mortal threat. It is narcissism as a medium for illusion, or narcissism supporting the ego ideal. It is narcissistic libido or primary anti-object and *ante*-object libido.

The compulsory theatre script between lovers has the first say, "You don't love me, you only love yourself!" To which the second answers, "You appear to love, but it's only so that you get back what you merely lend. You only love so that you're loved back." Writers such as Lacan have argued that the foundations of love are exclusively narcissistic. Nor is it not surprising that they cite the impossibility of surpassing hatred (*hainamoration*[28]).

No matter how deeply we delve into the question, we hit the bottom when we discover that the narcissistic limits of object-love are partially allied with hatred. But a single solution exists if we do not want to appear as mystics, and this is to intricate.

Narcissism *repels* death. It unseats, pursues, and harasses the death drive bent on conquering this first form of occupation (of investment) of the ego which aims at guaranteeing the support of Eros against the force whose intent is a turning back towards non-life. When the battle is done and over, then the sexual object libido may run through its cycle, oral followed by genital. At this point we find a "memory lapse" by Freud. He skips the anal phase, whereas he was the first to emphasise its close relationship to sadism, beginning with the Rat Man. This is perhaps because in this case he couldn't see that he held the missing link between the narcissistic libido and the *exteriorised* object libido in the training of the sphincter, which is bound to give up *ambivalent* dominance over the object.[29] Nor, moreover, does he say anything about the phallic stage.

What is important, despite this blind spot, is how Freud brings the role of narcissism into play, specifically, as a supporting scaffolding against the assaults of the death drive and about which it will no

---

[28] Translator's note: Lacan's portmanteau combining the French for "hatred" (*haine*) and "love" (*amour*).

[29] Cf. André Green, "Primary anality", in Green (2002).

longer be a question thereafter, life drives and death drives sharing the battlefield.

What Freud brings out for the first time is the close tie between the life (or love) drive, ego preservation, and the object, and at long last the avatars of the object investments whose backdrop is the key preoccupation of the object's protection by way of the twists and turns it encounters over time.

We then understand the post-Freudian slide which appears merely interested in object relations, whereas in truth the protection of the object at all costs is in sight as a manifestation of the life and love drives. And in the end, it's object-love that must be protected at any cost by the *supremacy of the life and love drives*. This bears noting: *there exists no recourse in the least to psychology, observations of the mother-child relationship, or developmental approaches*. It is truly a matter of metapsychology, or better, of a new metapsychology. I thus suggest, so as to differentiate it from that of 1915, calling it the "final metapsychology" by analogy with the "final drive theory".

Thus, in fact, we must lend our attention to such narcissism as *propping up*, all the while avoiding two errors. The first is denying its existence in favour of an initial and immediate object relation. The second is having it play a role which exempts us from seeing how the final drive theory now enables a dismantling of the scaffolding in order to make it possible to observe the changes that one may surmise through object transformations. Nor must one think that all has been said. Freud still has to touch up the key concepts which allow for the mythological surveys he suggests so as to meld them into theory.

When Freud delves into what comes next in his development, only the life and death drives remain face to face. Narcissism, *henceforth dissolved into the life drives*, has vanished from the scene. Freud then proceeds with a remarkable theoretical *après-coup*. If he provides us with no new ideas, he nonetheless reinterprets those he had advanced previously.

With the oral stage he associates the object's *annihilation*. Such complete destruction doesn't involve any particular aggressiveness. It results from the object's *consumption*, a point of view previously defended by Ferenczi before Freud himself adopted it. The separation which follows seems to me to be a result of the gradual distinguishing between narcissistic and object libido, just as anality shows us.

Freud makes no allusion to it. We may only think of anality with the emergence of the conflicts between expulsion and retention, the clinically attestable appearance of the relationship between the aggressiveness of infantile sexuality (the anal sadistic stage) and the dispossession of faeces, its gift to the mother during the training of the sphincter. What is more is that the anal-object is specifically cherished when internal and an object of repulsion when it gets to being expelled. How can Freud have forgotten this, along with the phallic stage and its dominant aggressive component?

He then comes to the stage of genital primacy, in which the object is directly concerned. Here we detect aggressiveness through the desire for ascendancy over the sexual object, ascendancy sometimes more symbolic than real, in order to testify to the male's supremacy. Freud then returns to drawing out his earlier speculation. The direction taken by the life drives follows the instruction of narcissism, which has evacuated the destructive drives outside the ego. The quest and investments of the object henceforth point the way to the object libido. The ego is no longer the most important focus of attention in thwarting death. The object assumes this position, despite being affected by ambivalence. Here then is a crucial observation: *it is object-love that becomes the most fundamental aim.* As soon as survival is assured and the foundations of the ego are established, object-love becomes the objective of the life drives, most likely because the aim of the libido, the fusion with another object, is what best expresses the vocation of the life drives; and surely, also, because object annihilations and the exchange between the ego and object give meaning to libidinal evolution. The life drives no longer solely depend on a drive goal but are also dependent on a relation to the other as other and object-supplement. The two forces nevertheless both subsist through the maintenance of ambivalence. Freud never postulated a beyond ambivalence or, better, a *beyond the life and death drives.* Too bad for the idealists.

1.4. The false symmetry of sadomasochism

S&M is the acronym by which one designates sadomasochism today. We need to go far back in Freud's oeuvre to find the traces of this coupling of a contrasting pair. The association occurs starting with the

Three Essays on Sexuality: "Sadism and masochism occupy a special position among the perversions, since the contrast between activity and passivity which lies behind them is among the universal characteristics of sexual life" (Freud, 1905, p. 159). But in the edition of 1924 Freud adds a note (Freud, 1905, p. 158, note 2) putting an end to this false symmetry by specifying that he now conceives the existence of a *primary erotogenic masochism*: "Sadism which cannot find employment in actual life is turned round upon the subject's own self and so produces a *secondary* masochism, which is superadded to the primary kind."

From that point on we observe that the sadism-masochism pair of opposites is no longer conceivable in this form. Before this addition, the "Papers on metapsychology" of 1915 revisit the 1905 interaction. The final drive theory (1920) considers primary sadism and primary masochism separately, the latter entitled to special treatment in "The economic problem of masochism" (Freud, 1924). We have already shown how the attacks of primary sadism bear on the initial organisation of the life drives, narcissism. What has survived these attacks, and which was not diverted towards the outside in the form of aggressiveness, remains in the ego and constitutes a deadly residue which is the lifelong support of the individual's self-destructive tendencies. Here Freud specifies: "Thus masochism appears to us in the light of a great danger, which is in no way true of its counterpart, sadism" (Freud, 1924, p. 159). In other words, sadism kills the other, but masochism kills the subject. This is why the affirmation that the pleasure principle is our life's guardian and not only our psyche's is reiterated.[30] Freud concludes with an earlier idea which identifies unpleasure with a state of tension and pleasure with relaxation. The qualitative factor henceforth recovers its rights: there exist pleasant tension and unpleasant relaxation. Freud (Freud, 1924, p. 160) then defines the function of three principles: Nirvana, associated with death; pleasure, with the libido's demands; and reality, with the outside world. "None of these three principles is actually put out of action by another" (Freud, 1924, p. 161). We are leaving out a development in which Freud expounds on

---

[30] Translator's note: Green is alluding here to Rosenberg (1999).

the examples of supposedly feminine masochism, nor will we go into the details of the feminine and moral forms of primary masochism. In "The economic problem of masochism", Freud repeats and makes his thinking clear:

> After the main portion of it has been transposed outwards on to objects, there remains inside, as a residuum of it, the eroto-genic masochism proper, which on the one hand has become a component of the libido and, on the other, still has the self as its object. This masochism would thus be evidence of, and a remainder from, the phase of development in which the coales-cence, which is so important for life, between the death drive and Eros took place.
>
> (Freud, 1924, p. 164)

He adds that sadism projected towards the outside "can be once more introjected, turned inwards, and in this way regress to its earlier situ-ation. If this happens, a secondary masochism is produced, which is added to the original masochism" (Freud, 1924, p. 164).

We see the difference between the version of 1920 in *Beyond the Plea-sure Principle* and that of 1924. In 1920, the accent was placed on pri-mary sadism, an effect of the destructive drive—the first drive—which aims at destroying the lineaments of Eros' narcissism established on the body proper. The residue of the death drive which could be evacuated towards the outside constitutes the self-destructive potential threaten-ing the individual. In 1924, priority is given to primary masochism. It is true that Freud recalls that "primary sadism is identical to masochism". But he is first and foremost concerned with original primary masoch-ism, which may give birth at a later time to a secondary masochism rein-trojected towards the inside. We can write out this process as follows:

> primary sadism = primary masochism → expulsion towards the outside—deadly residue → reintrojected projection—secondary masochism.

We observe how the fates of sadism and masochism differ. The symme-try of the primary is broken but the effects of primary masochism are a dangerous threat to the individual's survival, and not only to their psychic life. But, Freud concludes, "even the subject's destruction of himself cannot take place without libidinal satisfaction" (Freud, 1924, p. 170). Self-destruction is chained to Eros from which it cannot free itself.[31] The difficult question of drive renunciation must be asked here, and Freud goes into it in detail in *Discomfort in Culture*. What constitutes the primary (sadism or masochism) is the effect of the destruction and death drives. Eros is the shared enemy of both, the very Eros with which they may very well ally themselves in future.

1.5 Reworkings, advances, transpositions

What does Freud do after *Beyond the Pleasure Principle?* He first of all changes vertex. He immerses us in the depths of biological organisation and concludes with a psychoanalytic myth. As he cannot yet execute his programme, he changes course. He does so with *Group Psychology and the Analysis of the Ego* in which, lo and behold, at no time does he allude to the death drive even while his prescient thinking, unbeknownst to him, draws a picture of the rise and structure of Nazism. Already delineated is the problem of dealing with group phenomena and collective thinking as well as the role of the other in psychic life. There is still another moment of respite and then we finally come to *The Ego and the Id*, the reworking of the theorems and exposition of the new metapsychology. We will not linger over this but do little more than point out its novelties.

1) At the foundation of the psyche is the id, by way of the following steps:
   a) Withdrawal of the unconscious and its replacement by the id. That is, an overriding of the notion of the unconscious as a system in defence of the id. In the id, there is no reference of the concept of representation, not even unconscious.
   b) The fundamental element of the psyche is the drive motion.[32]

---

[31] Translator's note: Green is alluding to his work, *The Chains of Eros* (1997).
[32] Cf. our work, "From the Unconscious to the Id", in Green (2006b).

c) Drive dualism is distributed between life or love drives and death or destruction drives, bringing about tension or discharge.

2) The ego

The greatest part of the defences arising out of it are henceforth *unconscious*. Its principal expression is identification. The perceptual system and the triggering of anxiety further depend on it.

3) The superego

The new arrival in the system, produced out of a splitting within the ego, divided between the superego and the ego ideal. The superego is constituted by identification with the superego *of the parents*. A new mechanism tied to virtuality is inaugurated. Not an object relation but a relation to the (absent) object of the object. The superego sinks its roots into the id and is modifiable by regression. Like the id, it may be constituted by a destructive apportioning and by an apportioning of love, each in conflict with the other.

The introduction of the superego is revolutionary. It signals the impact of the cultural processes on the psychic apparatus, an effect of the oedipal and group processes beyond individual contentiousness. The superego condemns forbidden wishes, principally incestuous vows (of love) or parricide (of death).[33] As it is a matter of unconscious vows, it produces a feeling of guilt, which Freud prefers calling a consciousness of guilt or, better yet, the need for self-punishment. The intrication of the death drive and sexual function (built around the life drives) gives birth to primary masochism, which is composed of several forms (erotogenic, feminine, moral).

Here then is an important modification: *masochism is now first; it is the central expression of the death drive*; aggression is but the portion *projected onto the outside* (following the example of the narcissistic libido driving off primary sadism). The death drive henceforth takes refuge in the heart of the ego and cannot be fought against directly.

---

[33] By dint of our formulation, we are letting slide the differences between the two forms of Oedipus, the boy's and the girl's, in addition to the positive and negative Oedipus complexes. The problem surely warrants detailed study. To cite one example, parricide and matricide are not equivalents. The first is punished by castration while the second, by madness.

Only its intricated forms may become the object of an analysis, which in favourable developments will lead to its dissolution or its integration in the ego. The proof of the relative success of this operation is the existence of the negative therapeutic reaction. In my view, this is the decisive argument which must have brought about a change in Freud's opinion towards absolute certainty concerning the death drive. The argument isn't merely clinical but metapsychological. One can argue that the whole of "Analysis terminable and interminable" is devoted to this. We should add, however, that Freud's arguments are less decisive than he might think because techniques other than his may sometimes lead to better results. But there is no illusory optimism; the problem raised by Freud is not an artefact and has lost nothing of its import in our time.

The Ego and the Id has been better received by the analytic community than *Beyond the Pleasure Principle*, though not without a few reservations: "Yes, but without the death drive"—a veritable wrecker of the analyst's self-confidence. Analysts shed tears over the time when they had a suitably accommodating first topography at their disposal: nothing could replace the unconscious–preconscious–conscious triad. And still more, if the ego is unconscious of its own resistances, who can one trust? The superego is without doubt useful, but it is more often understood as resulting from the relationship to the parents. Generally speaking, the analytic community seems to think, "Try a little harder and there will be no doubt as to the fact that we'll be analysts once we rid ourselves of this metaphysical stench!" They are poor tinkerers of a simplified, naive reality. Freud wages the battle and carries on. His programme must be carried through to its completion. He returns to the Oedipus complex, theorised at last—which he was unable to do before *Totem and Taboo*—,deepens its foundations, and considers its fate, and even its decline. Admittedly, it was about time that he went into the relation of the theory to certain clinical problems such as the guilty conscience, understandable henceforth by way of the superego. This is when, in 1924 with "The economic problem of masochism", he reached the end of a reflection first taken up in 1895. After Sabina Spielrein and Barbara Low, from this point forward he sorts the principles of psychic functioning according to three axes:

1) Low's principle of Nirvana, the aspiration of a zero level of libidinal excitation (Nirvana); this must be related to the death drive *without being accessible to the individual's psychic investigation*. It is linked to the old principle of inertia from 1895 and the hypothesis on the death drive in *Beyond the Pleasure Principle*.

2) The modification of the preceding *among living beings* and its replacement by the pleasure principle, which recalls the earlier constancy principle and is accessible to clinical investigation.

3) A new modification of the preceding among the most complex living beings under the influence of reality. The reality principle is the safeguard of the pleasure principle. It is the cause of frustration, but also the condition for viable psychic life.

This novel classification explains that we as human beings are dealing with none other than the pleasure principle–reality principle pair. But the residual effects of the death drive oblige Freud to envisage its pernicious and infinitely dangerous role, which for him is never directly observable[34] in its pure state. The fundamental relationship of both the life and death drives is their presence in the *intricated* state, or as the result of disintrication, that is, fused or defused. There may then become comprehensible its three aspects designated by Freud as exemplary, namely, the guilty conscience, masochism, and the negative therapeutic reaction.

We may now understand the advantage of making a recourse to myth. By means of the perspective that it made possible and the speculations that it succeeded in expressing, it opened up a pathway towards clinical practice. The myth supplied an initial vision which begins with biology and reaches, through the development of its own (psychic) means, individual evolution, doubtless starting with the Oedipus complex which isn't reducible to an individual developmental approach. *Totem and Taboo* directs us towards an anthropological path.

Freud believed that he had carried out his programme of 1920. This is surely so, but 1921 looms on the horizon since *Group Psychology and the Analysis of the Ego* calls for an exploration of a new order. The life and

---

[34] With a few exceptions.

death drives continue to play their role but *at a different level*, an anthropological one. Once again, myth is called on in exploring this field.

The return to myth is thus the return to a primal state of thinking which may take two paths: first, the biological one leading to the crowning of infantile sexuality; and second, the anthropological one leading to the theorising of groups and culture. What then remains is thinking about this in *Discomfort in Culture* and lastly, his work's final say, *The Man Moses and Monotheistic Religion*. At this point he needs to make use of clinical practice, but without being subjugated to it, and to be sufficiently steadfast in order to pursue the speculation by opening it up to new fields of knowledge. There can be no doubt that without the creation of the superego none of this would have been possible. Pushing the theory of the superego up to the venture of the death drive remains a necessity.

The clinical merit of the questions that Freud asks beginning in 1920 and their relation to the "Papers on metapsychology" of 1915 are now resolved, even if quarrels rage in psychoanalytic circles concerning the validity of the explanations of the founder of psychoanalytic theory. What still remains for us to do is to recall Freud's revisions of two of his postulates. The first ties unpleasure to an excess of tensions which are neither dischargeable nor repressible. But now (in 1924), Freud recognises that there exist pleasurable tension and unpleasurable relaxation. Henceforth, quality poses a problem independent of its relationship to quantity. The second is the discovery by Freud of splitting, in his 1927 essay concerning fetishism, with the illustration of a process of *disavowal* which splits the child's ego when he refuses to decide in favour of fantasy or reality, that is, to adopt a solution which contributes to disuniting it. Freud admits the coexistence of these two contradictory responses, at once yes and no, decisively creating a breach in the ego's unity and whose involvement in non-neurotic structures, principally perverse and psychotic, is patent.

One might say that by 1929 the programme of 1920 was wrapped up. And yet Freud did not stop there. He recalled that the reference to the drives' action cannot be satisfied by a strictly individual or familial (oedipal) approach. Beginning in 1929, he opens up a new field of research which in 1930 leads to his landmark work, *Discomfort in Culture*.

Freud transposes his field of investigation onto society and henceforth sees the elective domain of the death drive within it. For culture can only be founded through drive renunciation. The sacrifice agreed on by this abandoning, far from being satisfied with producing compensatory effects of a narcissistic order, in return arouses a reaction of protest against this renunciation. The field of culture becomes the arena in which are developed the most destructive effects of the death drive. Laurence Kahn (2005) has granted its full importance to this course, and it is doubtless not a coincidence if she counts among the uncommon writers who understand the necessity of the concept of the death drive. Nathalie Zaltzman and Jean-Luc Donnet have also discussed the consequences of this "transference" by Freud (cf. Donnet & Zaltzman, 2003).

Freud's opus thus closes with the parricide of Moses, but, strange to say, here Freud delivers a final message in which is found conjoined what one may relate to the effects of the death drive on the individual and collective levels, and yet he *doesn't say a word on this subject*. He keeps quiet about the concept. I do not think that he would have hesitated from bringing the hypothesis into play. On the other hand, I believe that he was sufficiently preoccupied by the future of psychoanalytic theory to refrain from voicing what he thought of it. He accepted taking risks vis-à-vis the public but perhaps feared rejection by his own.[35]

1.6 Conclusion: Transcendence in Freud

Freud, an anti-philosophical writer and yet a philosopher despite himself, asks the question concerning the existence of a transcendental polarity in his work. There is no doubt that he would not have wished to see himself in it. Did he not express his thinking with sufficient clarity with regard to the *Weltanschauung* in 1933? The sphere of his labour was science and science alone. René Thom, who in his preface to the

---

[35] The following is a piece of evidence in support of this idea. In the *Letters of Sigmund Freud and Karl Abraham, 1907–1926*, Freud asserts that he and Abraham have always got along splendidly and further that Abraham regularly received all of Freud's manuscripts. In light of our present reading, we see how Abraham reacts quite favourably to "The unhomely" and makes a great many interesting comments concerning *Group Psychology and the Analysis of the Ego*. This concerns those works which precede and immediately follow *Beyond the Pleasure Principle*. Yet Abraham confirms that he has received Freud's text of 1920 though never makes any mention of it, whether positively or negatively. Was his silence not intended to show his disapproval? Cf. Freud and Abraham (1965).

Encyclopædia Universalis is more scientific than Freud but more rigorous as a critic of science, entitles his article, "Science, despite it all."

Freud cannot bear being included among the cadres of thinking in principle conceived in order to exclude him. But he himself, all the while refusing alternative solutions, often behaves in an antiscientific way, as for example when he refuses the limitations that Darwin's theory against Lamarck's imposes on him. The argument is variable: "I'm a psychoanalyst, not a scholar." In other words, "Never mind, you'll catch up with me later." Should we posit the hypothesis of transcendence in Freud, it isn't in order to give answers which would force open a door which remains closed. "No, there isn't any transcendence in Freud's work." To which we reply: "Yes, there is not *one* but *two* transcendences which command this one-of-a-kind work." There are thus two pillars, beyond Freudian therapeutics. The first, fundamental for him, results from our condition as *living human beings*. Its origin is thus found at the biological or, rather, *metabiological* level. It assures the relationship of psychoanalysis to the natural sciences. It calls for a reflection on life going back to the lowest forms, which are then passed on to human beings. Here Freud is closer to Darwin. What is human doesn't surpass the living, the latter continuing to play an active role in it.

The second pillar, just as fundamental as the preceding even if it was discovered *later*, is anthropological. It is guided by the principle that the living human being is human and living in equal parts. What is sure is that what appertains to humans in their own right is that which connects them to life. Anthropology is defined with difficulty but it opens up the chapter of a particularity. The anthropological vision predicates that the relation of one human being to another is as fundamental as that which connects human beings to life, for without taking this point of view into consideration the living human being ceases to be human. The *Umwelt* of man (von Weizsäcker) isn't restricted to defining man's environment as consisting in his world. This *Umwelt* is first and foremost a human *Umwelt*, and even the world of the *physis* is, further, a psychological world which is the acquisition of that which makes what is living human. This is what is at the heart of the deepest analytic relationship. But we ought to be wary and tell ourselves that what is human is singular in its humanity but also double—masculine and feminine—without being entirely dissociable from its ties to what is animal.

Biology and anthropology do not come under the relationship to life alone. They must further include—in relation to the mortal and living human being—that which is immortalised by culture. This is what the Freudian reflection on the death drive teaches us, and which wound up taking over the world of culture.

Note on Empedocles of Acragas

At the end of his opus, so as to shore up his position, Freud makes reference to Empedocles, notably in "Analysis terminable and interminable" (1937). Empedocles, then, since Empedocles there is—there is in fact only him—and yet is he a benchmark by whom one is honoured in mentioning him? Nothing is less certain since, as we shall see, he arouses very divided opinions.

Grandson of an Olympic champion likewise called Empedocles; a statesman and democratic despite coming from the aristocracy, and who is said to have refused the royalty which he was offered; a thaumaturgic doctor with a contested reputation; a partisan of pluralism (starting from the four elements: fire, air, water, and earth) and naturalist theories. He was interested, just as was Freud, in sensation and the theory of knowledge, and keen on reducing the physical and psychic phenomena of humans, animals, and plants to natural universal processes. Such is this archaic philosopher—about whom some dispute that he deserves this qualification (Kojève). We cannot wholly count on him without criticising him. Some associate him with the Pythagoreans. We possess more fragments by him than any other pre-Socratic philosopher. He expresses his thinking in verse and is supposed to have been one of the founders of rhetoric. His philosophy deals with diverse themes. In this connection, he doesn't spare himself from stating nonsense like that which claims, according to Varro, that men sprouted out of the earth like spinach (autochthony) or that individuals are either born male or female depending on heat—men are warm—or coolness—women are cold. He also held a high opinion of himself and took himself for a god. Aristotle, who cited him often, qualified his thoughts as "stammering".

For Freud, however, he remains the theorist who comes to the rescue of his final drive theory:

> now coming together by Love all into one,
> now again all being carried apart by the hatred of Strife.
> (In Barnes, 2001, p. 121)

Likewise, he had the intuition of what Freud would maintain as drive intrication and disintrication. Love and hate are principles, not causes:

> In Anger they have different forms and are all apart,
> but in Love they come together and are desired by one another.
> (In Barnes, 2001, p. 128)

These verses are drawn from Simplicius' *Commentary on the Physics* by Aristotle. John Burnet summarises this point as follows: "The function of Love is to produce union; that of Strife, to break it up again" (Burnet, 1920, p. 232). Love is only capable of deploying its effects when Hatred divides the Sphere. Thus, as in Freudian theory, Love outlasted Hatred.

Aristotle maintained that the world had found itself in the era of Hatred. I cannot say what direct knowledge, or through the accounts of the Greek authors, Freud had of pre-Socratic philosophy. As he himself reveals, Theodor Gomperz—who wrote of Empedocles, "the merit of the doctrine was incalculable" (Gomperz, 1901, p. 232)—introduced him to his ideas.[36]

But Burnet doesn't hesitate with calling him a charlatan. As to Alexandre Kojève, the antithetical parathesis which would reconcile Parmenides (Empedocles was his student) and Heraclitus—the Sphere and the River—is a monstrosity. In fact, the predominant Heraclitean feature is perceptible. Kojève (1968, p. 268*f*) founds his analysis on the notion of cycle—contested by Jean Bollack (1965–1969).

In Empedocles, the inconsistencies are not wanting. A pluralist (the four elements), he did not establish an unshakable distinction between the inanimate world and the organic world, no more than he separated nature and soul (cf. Barnes, 2001).

---

[36] Freud knew him personally. Cf. Gomperz (1901).

He endows the four elements with divine nature. The soul is a daemon propelled outside its natural destination. It is a bearer of primal guilt through the blood it shed and the false oath it executed. Driven from its original habitation, it is forbidden from returning to it. In any case, not before ten thousand years. Whence the work on *Purifications*. The idea of a soul which is separated from the body was attributed to Alfred von Kremer who, after in-depth investigations into Oriental thinking, maintained that vapour was born of recently spilled warm blood and then ascended to heaven, which is the source of the idea of the soul as breath ("pneuma").[37] The seat of the soul is the heart. Empedocles— in contrast with Lucretius—thus shares the idea of an immortal soul. The discrepancy is situated between the materialist idea (the scientific outlook) and the religious idea (steeped in Orphism). Freud was doubtless seduced by this scientific reference and saw himself in Empedocles as a thinker of movement. If he was close to Pythagoras, Parmenides, and Anaxagoras, he defended the ideas of the thinker of Ionia.

Empedocles ended his days in exile, not far from Agrigento. The version of his death by suicide—he threw himself into Etna, one of his sandals was found near the pits of the volcano—seems assuredly fabulous, just like the life of this precursor of Freud.

---

[37] Discussed by Theodor Gomperz, in Gomperz (1901).

CHAPTER 2

The death drive's shockwave: Ferenczi, Melanie Klein, Bion, Winnicott, Lacan, and others

Remarks on some clinical structures

2.1 Ferenczi and mutual analysis

Freud's legacy is divided into several currents each of which adopts a different position on the death drive. There are those—they comprise the greatest number—who give no credence to it and seek substitute concepts, which all turn out to be blunt-sided. Ferenczi introduces a new way of practising analysis without nevertheless offering an opinion. Then there are those, among whom one counts Melanie Klein, who feel they are continuing Freud's work by orientating it towards the search for fixations going back to the first stages of development. From that point on, the essential preoccupation consists in defining oneself in relation to Melanie Klein. Some, such as Bion, develop Klein's ideas and define them with greater rigour. They persist in subscribing to the hypothesis of the destruction and death drive. Still others, all the while acknowledging the importance of Klein, distinguish themselves in relation to her thinking. Here I have in mind Winnicott. There are, further, those who accept a drive theory but replace the death drive with aggressiveness. This is the North American position led by Heinz Hartmann. Lastly, Jacques Lacan, having long flirted with death—the Absolute Master—, increasingly says nothing about it in his theory, even though the Lacanian movement is engaged in a destructive fight with its opponents. To top it all off, there is yet a final current which has had enough of hearing any talk about drives, whether life drives and still less death drives. No one can say that Freud has been honoured by his children! Let's kill the death drive and we'll survive in peace! These days, fashion grants favour to the relational current, including object relations (Fairbairn and Klein), relational analysis (Greenberg and Mitchell), and pragmatic relational analysis (Renik). All that remains is to bury Freud once and for all. Happily, though, such isn't the case in France.

We have already commented on the "coincidence" in 1924 of the debates on Freudian clinical practice and technique, one year after the appearance of *The Ego and the Id*. The protagonists include Otto Rank, whose theory replacing Freud's will not endure for long, and especially Sándor Ferenczi who, by focusing more on technical questions in a series of works dated from 1927 to 1933, had more followers. Even more than these contributions, some of which became famous in their own right, the *Clinical Diary*, which covers the year 1932, goes to the very crux of the matter.

The whole of this period was marked by Freud's and Ferenczi's troubled relationship. However much the latter tried to pledge his loyalty to Freud, Freud sensed his friend and collaborator distance himself from him. The question may be asked differently today. Was Ferenczi correct, in light of the most recent psychoanalytic experience, in rattling the Freudian edifice despite the reality? "Not in front of the children!" say the squabbling parents, as if their children had not long sensed better than the aforementioned parties themselves that divorce was in the air. The fact remains that those close to Ferenczi advised against the publication of the *Clinical Diary* until after his death, while waiting for the mood to calm. Even though he died in 1933, Ferenczi's contributions only reached the public in 1955. The third volume of Jones' Freud biography, in which Jones launches an attack on him, appeared in 1957. Set to appear in 1969, the publication of the *Clinical Diary* was delayed until 1985. Ferenczi is treated as no better than a dissident, as if he had merged with Jung, Adler, and Stekel. I am convinced that Freud, were he alive, would have refused this politicking, so violent was the conflict between his biographer and his "paladin".[38] Freud knew that he could at the very least count on Ferenczi's integrity, if not his orthodoxy.

Ferenczi's *Clinical Diary* lets off a poignant resonance, that of the cry of a man caught between the desire to keep on being himself despite the dangerous price to pay and the necessity of coming down on the side of Freud so as not to lose his love.

With Ferenczi is introduced:

1) Psychoanalytic clinical practice centred on the ego and extended to a reparative technique.
2) A shift in emphasis to the countertransference.

Ferenczi is assuredly not lacking in perspicuity with regard to Freud, but he is overwhelmed by a demand for unconditional love which keeps him from giving up on Freud's approval. I am in no way exaggerating when I insist that the question of the death drive is what is left unspoken in their disagreement. But what is important are the technical measures devised in order to contend with it. Ferenczi wishes to recognise the deadly effects of the destruction drive when he emphasises the disappearance of the somatic phenomena of self-preservation. On 10 January 1932, he writes in his *Clinical Diary*, "he [the patient] is no longer worried about breathing or about the preservation of his life in general. Moreover, he regards being destroyed or mutilated with interest, as if it is no longer his own self but another person who is undergoing these torments" (Ferenczi, 1932, p. 6). Indifference is a way of taking vengeance against the sadist. What I have described as *excorporation* then occurs (Green, 1990). The splitting and atomising of psychic life become sought-after psychic defences. Ferenczi demonstrates how the patient exploits his or her masochism. The end of the session destroys the acquisitions that this had made possible.

Ferenczi's position is ambivalent. On the one hand, he recognises the trace in the pathology of what Freud argues with the idea of the death drive, but, on the other hand, he attributes its responsibility to the parents. Freud will criticise Ferenczi's excessive belief in the reality

---

[38] Freud described Ferenczi as the "paladin" of psychoanalysis.

described by the patient. Mutual analysis contributes to this defence by reality: "It's the other who ..." Then again, Ferenczi recognises the predominance of the pleasure principle. On this occasion, he invokes the case of masochism: suffering as source of satisfaction. This however doesn't exclude the implementation of sadistic drives. In fact, Ferenczi's technique transforms analysis into a breeding ground and leads, as he writes on 3 March 1932, to the "terrorism of suffering" (Ferenczi, 1932, p. 47).

Ferenczi remained committed to technical problems, whereas Freud wanted him to turn away from this path and accept the presidency of the International Psychoanalytical Association in order to settle the political problems of the time. But, coinciding with the subterranean activating of his guilty feeling, Ferenczi's health deteriorated. Judith Dupont (1988) accurately summarises the three matters at hand: the hypotheses on trauma, the response given to them by *mutual analysis*, and lastly the frame's "trial", to use Raymond Cahn's expression (1983).

A turning point in analysis has been reached. The patient suffers less from fixations than traumas left unanswered, from the hypocrisy of adults which is then transferred onto that of society, and then onto that of the analyst in the treatment. The drive-force of aggression is no longer the cause of neurosis but rather the consequences of the trauma which generates the defensive retreat of the patient, who adopts a distorted vision vis-à-vis the aggressor. It is essential that the analyst accepts what is at times a caricatured take on things in order to recognise its underlying reality in the face of which all others remain mute. Ferenczi is alluding less to his experience as Freud's analysand than to that of his own patients' analyst.

Time and again we go back to the preponderant place of self-criticism. Freud would surely see in it an effect of the guilty conscience, a solution which leaves Ferenczi dissatisfied. In a nutshell, at the root of trauma Ferenczi sees the perpetuation of the parents' hypocrisy in the confusion of tongues. Heralding Winnicott, he considers of utmost importance submitting the frame to criticism, and thereby becomes the advocate of lost causes. We might inquire what this technique includes as an unconscious return to the past. Isn't Ferenczi bringing back up the merits of the pre-1897 *trauma theory* once again? He maximises the role of trauma and speaks in favour of an "organic hysteria" in which is expressed the role of *body-thinking* and its vicissitudes. Added to this is a fatal incapacity on the part of the analyst-parent to respond to it; in other words, an inevitable deficiency of the environment. A negative transference generates an overcompensation which the analyst interprets as an amorous countertransference. The analyst, frightened by this reaction, withdraws his or her libido from the countertransference, which produces the belated becoming into consciousness of the analyst's negative countertransference and which leads to an intensified return of overcompensation.

Here we observe a dilemma. An attitude of pushing the limits of neutrality is supposed to prevent this turmoil. What is needed is returning to the early beginnings of the treatment by giving up neutrality, which turns out to be an obstacle for mobilising the neurosis's organisation. We should note, however, that most of the cases reported by Ferenczi are women and they pose the problem of the hysteric component in their pathology, even if it was "organic" hysteria. Mutual analysis, which Ferenczi believes is the solution to all these difficulties, should wind up generating more positive than harmful effects.

How does mutual analysis allow for the analysis of transference? In a surprising way, it appears that rationalisation takes hold of the analyst's theoretical constructions. The failure of this technique ended up by being correct about it. One may nevertheless ask if present-day *disclosure* doesn't represent the naive return of an experiment which in the past had shown its limitations. Ferenczi was seeking a solution to the impasse—how not to outdo his master—of his own analysis with Freud. Giving the Freud–Ferenczi debate a reading pays off. It explains how it led to a dead-end, when there came into play an analytic impasse which was the expression of a quasi-psychotic transference. Ferenczi was very near to being conscious of this and he understood how he was caught up in such a situation with Freud. And what if we were simply dealing with a case of negative therapeutic reaction which went unnoticed by the object of the transference, that is, Freud? This is what Freud's allusion to Ferenczi in "Analysis terminable and interminable", written after the death of the Hungarian, indicates.

This amounts to recognising the effect of the transference—with the risk of overlooking the resistance *of* transference. The repetition compulsion is brought into question on this occasion. Resistance makes use of it in order to take the opportunity to work it through: "[What] is the use of [repeating] the trauma word for word, to have the same disillusionment with the whole world and the whole of humanity?" (10 March 1932, in Ferenczi, 1932, p. 55).

Ferenczi insists on the right to express his disappointment vis-à-vis the patient in order to attain a more positive transference. Mutual analysis teaches us that it does not in the least diminish the role of the most unconscious fantasies. He recognises that he never succeeded in obtaining the rememoration of the traumatic processes themselves by means of this technique.

Ferenczi substantiates the desire for death among some children—which explains the sacrificial postures of the analyst in mutual analysis. He experiences disillusion and on 31 March 1932 writes: "Disquieting idea that the patient has succeeded in escaping from analysis entirely, and in taking me into analysis instead" (Ferenczi, 1932, p. 73).

The "immersion" has to go back to the intrauterine situation, which expresses the omnipotence of mothers, which does not fail to assimilate part of the victim through identification. All hatred is projection which protects from pain, this bringing to mind projective identification which will only later be defined by Melanie Klein. On the other hand, the drive side of infantile sexuality is but the reversal of the passionate violence of adults leading to the confusion of tongues artificially implanted in children. Ferenczi comes to an entirely new construction of the infantile psyche and in doing so paves the way for Winnicott's thinking.

A question Ferenczi raises is that which we ourselves would like to raise: "Who is crazy, we or the patients?" (1 May 1932, in Ferenczi, 1932, p. 92).[39] This challenging of the adults' health necessarily leads to a criticism of Freud who, according to Ferenczi, remains intellectually attached to analysis despite his many disappointments but not emotionally so since he complies with a superego not unlike that of a researcher in natural sciences. Freud, in brief, does not really like his patients; nor is he prepared to grant them the sacrifices that Ferenczi accepts.

---

[39] "The children or the adults?" "[Why] then should he, the patient, place himself blindly in the power of the doctor?" (Ferenczi, 1932, p. 92).

The latter was courageous enough to relate his difficulties to his own infantile experience and the guilt-inducing role of the mother.

In a sense, Ferenczi pushes a certain psychoanalytic ideology to the point of absurdity. Since the analyst cannot analyse what remains unanalysed in himself, he's constrained to becoming the analysand of the analysand, as if the patient were capable of neutrality and could renounce taking advantage of the opportunity which is thereby handed to him for brutalising the analyst *as in the situation leading to an amorous acting-out.* In some cases, splitting divides an entirely indifferent observing ego and an affectively implicated ego. Rememoration cannot be merely the manifestation of traumatic scars—*always having an external origin*—of the psyche seeking to face up to the *kill or be killed* pair. Getting to the bottom of things means making ourselves available to the patient in a "passionately active" way. Passionately, following the example of Jesus Christ's passion. Mutual analysis ought to conclude with mutual forgiveness.

Alright, then, *basta!* What interests us today is Ferenczi's opening of a new clinical field and the description of transferential forms "at the limits of the analysable".[40] This is why the question doesn't come to an end with Ferenczi's passing but continues in analysis in our own time, with Winnicott's theory. The problem remains whole: that of the limits of the analysable and the technical modifications defensible when working with non-neurotic structures. This situation is not unrelated to the current preference given by some writers with regard to the psychoanalytic face-to-face configuration. It is of significance that with Ferenczi an alternative to drive theory is opened up in which a continually developing relational theory may be perceived in embryonic form. The intersubjective dimension overtakes the intrapsychic dimension. The modifications of the intrapsychic are always the result of intersubjective effects. But what of the situation between two subjects? Ferenczi's failings lie in the revenge of the intrapsychic and the confirmation that Freud's point of view wasn't surpassed. It's doubtless necessary to arrive

---

[40] The title of Number 10 of the *Nouvelle Revue de Psychanalyse* (New Review of Psychoanalysis) published prior to the 1975 International Psychoanalytical Association (IPA) congress held in London.

at a new idea of the relationship between the two in order to give treatment any chance for success.

2.2 Melanie Klein and generalised destructiveness

Melanie Klein first underwent analysis with Ferenczi. Dissatisfied with her experience, she undertook a second one with Abraham, which better suited her.[41] She had no difficulty in formulating her own system of thinking as she had acquired firm convictions. She however scarcely cites writers other than Freud of whom manifestly, as she was setting out, she wished to be the rightful heir. Giving an account of the Kleinian system from its beginnings up through our time is no simple task. Elizabeth Bott Spillius (1988) may guide the interested reader along this route.

We will limit ourselves to addressing the points that concern the death drive. Klein, in fact, is distinguished from other psychoanalysts by her unreserved adherence to the death drive. If she happens to contest Freud, it is certainly not for the excessive way that he uses the final drive theory. It is rather for greatly restricting the views for which she conceived a very broad application.

Her elective fields are the psychoanalysis of children and seriously regressed adults. Let's state it straight away: theory, as passionate as it is, interests her less than technique and clinical practice with children, which at the time had largely to be developed and posed problems as to the adaptation of the technique used with adults. Her attention was drawn to the importance of the early interpretation of the negative transference, a transference which is no different, in her view, from the adult's, which is to be interpreted in depth. This transference is expressed by an overtly perceptible fear.

Klein takes a bit of time before she works out her theory, which she then expounds repetitively and whenever the occasion presents itself. Kleinian theory is based very broadly—seeing itself in line with the last Freud—on the predominance of the destructive drives over the erotic drives. The search for pleasure is only secondary and defensive

---

[41] Melanie Klein dedicated *The Psychoanalysis of Children* (1932a), her first book, to him.

in relation to the preoccupation with neutralising the effects of the destructive drives.

The initial structured theoretical developments date to 1928 and Klein's chapter on "Early stages of the Oedipus conflict and of super-ego formation" (Klein, 1932b) returns to and expands on these themes. For Klein, the oedipal conflict arises during the middle of the first year of existence and lasts until the third year. She follows Abraham: pleasure in suckling at the beginning followed by pleasure in biting (the second oral sub-stage). At times there exists inhibition deriving from an abnormally heightened oral sadism. Notwithstanding, a particularly robust libido may precede a frustration and its inhibition. It is thus the premature appearance of sadism which is harmful. In her view, ego-development has an edge on the libido's development. The consequent frustration is accompanied by anxiety due to "the accumulation of stimuli which require to be discharged" (Freud, 1926, quoted in Klein, 1932b, p. 182[42]), an assertion reiterated by Bion. The child's fears converge on the external object, a position that development will dissipate with the reality which recognises the "good mother" and which replaces the object's destruction through its conservation. As with Freud, there exists a by-passing of the death drive towards the exterior. But at the same time, internal dangers are constituted beside those originating in the outside. Oral sadism attains its apogee during and after weaning. Directed against the mother's breast, it spreads throughout the inside of the entirety of her body.

It is, however, through urethral sadism that oral sadism perpetuates itself. The child—inundated, submerged, burned, and poisoned—releases great quantities of urine against the mother, avenging him- or herself thereby for the frustration that she inflicted (enuresis, games with the penis). The penis is invested with cruel activity, which reverberates onto the sexual function and inhibits it. Oral-sadistic desires are associated with anal-sadistic desires: "their primal aim of eating up and destroying her breast is always discernible in them" (Klein, 1932b, p. 187).

---

[42] Translator's note: The *Standard Edition* renders this phrase, from *Inhibitions, Symptoms and Anxiety*, as the "accumulation of amounts of stimulation which require to be disposed of" (Freud, 1926, p. 137).

We observe that the phallic stage is essentially sadistic. On this point Klein aligns herself with Abraham:

> I know from my own experience, to bring oneself to recognise such an abhorrent idea answers to the truth. But the abundance, force and multiplicity of the imaginary cruelties which accompany these cravings are displayed before our eyes in early analyses so clearly and forcibly that they leave no room for doubt.
>
> (Klein, 1932b, pp. 187–188)

Freud's "true" daughter takes over his positions. We recall the date, 1932, the year of the essays from Ferenczi's final period and in particular, "Confusion of tongues between adults and the child".

Aligning herself thereby with Abraham, Klein argues that the pleasure drawn by the nursling from these sadistic satisfactions is not uniquely due to the libido but is tied to a violent appetite for destruction "which aims at the injury or annihilation of its object" (Klein, 1932b, p. 187). This is presumed to take place between six and twelve months of age. This situation leads to the *intensification* of sadism due to the frustration related to the impossibility of satisfying libidinal needs. The attacks spread out to the father's penises (in the plural, since he has many available) incorporated by the mother. He becomes the most redoubtable destructive agent. According to Klein, the father plays a very important role in the aetiology of mental disturbances. But, we should note, solely in the form of penis-incorporated-in-the-belly of the mother and comprising with her the fantasy of the combined parent.

Concerning the primal scene, sadism is encountered as dreaded for the death wishes that it engenders, and which give rise to exacerbated mutual destruction, the sign of mistreatment exchanged between the two partners: the penis becomes a dangerous animal or loaded with explosive arms while the vagina is simultaneously imagined as a poisonous witch.

An oedipal dynamic is established:

> According to my view, the Oedipus conflict sets in the boy as soon as he begins to have feelings of hatred against his father's

penis and to want to achieve genital union with his mother and destroy his father's penis which he imagines to be inside her body.

(Klein, 1932b, p. 191)

For Klein, the genital drives appear at the same time as the pre-genital drives, and thus do not follow them. This destructiveness eventually engenders reparative guilt. For this is a merciless war which takes place earlier and is accompanied by vengeful fantasies on the part of the parents.

The sense of guilt with regard to genital masturbatory fantasies derives from the sadistic fantasies directed against the parents and not from their incestuous content (Klein, 1932b, p. 193). Klein bases herself here on the quotation of Freud concerning the precession of hatred over love, as well as on other excerpts treating the dissolution of the Oedipus complex, on *Inhibitions, Symptoms and Anxiety* and, lastly, on *The Ego and the Id*. There can be no doubt that she has read Freud thoroughly but, as she herself says, she prefers a simpler and more direct process (Klein, 1932b, p. 195). In other words, the superego is precociously erected against the destructive drives. The matter is all the more inevitable as these drives are diverted towards the outside, that is, towards the object, as they may uniquely arouse hostility in return through a mechanism having phylogenetic roots. "[I]n no period of life is the opposition between ego and superego so strong as in early childhood" (Klein, 1932b, p. 198). Freud spoke out against this view. In fact, Melanie Klein bases herself—contrary to Freud—exclusively on endopsychic processes. The relations of the ego with objects are reproduced through subsequent relations between the superego and ego, which Freud had earlier maintained in 1915 in "Mourning and melancholia" (1917).

Isn't Klein's interpretation influenced by her reference models, including paranoid projection, schizophrenia, hypochondria, and catatonia? We should recall their privileged tie with narcissism. Concerning anality, the interpretation of the role played by excrement as a projectile endowed with immense destructive capacities is grossly "conveyed". Such an object isn't found in a single form but is reproduced in myriad specimens. Possession within the body represents possession of the external mother and "symbolises the external world and reality" (Klein, 1932b, p. 208). It is worth recalling that Klein likewise mentions the role played by the (erotic) libido and the influence of reality. This is a feeble counterweight at the root of which will be termed the "good object".

Melanie Klein next brings these observations together and describes the two great position characteristic of infantile sexuality. First, the paranoid–schizoid position, marked in the child by persecutory positions and deep annihilation (*néantisation*) anxiety arousing splitting, denial, idealisation, and omnipotence, and which are contemporary with the emergence of paranoid anxieties accompanying an experience of splitting up, fragmentation, and the destructive attacks of the part-object. This is followed by the depressive position which starts with the beginnings of object unification in which one observes the appearance of the sense of guilt together with the desire for the reparation of damages brought about by it, a feeling of responsibility for the destructive devastation. The separation between the paranoid–schizoid position and the depressive position was warranted by evolution, the second succeeding the first. This sequence will be challenged later and the opinion of the Kleinians will incline towards a simultaneity (repeating itself several times over) of the two positions. The role of introjection and projection will be clarified. Drive motions and unconscious fantasies are in fact only two sides of a single reality. Fantasies are the expression of the drive (Susan Isaacs). Kleinian psychopathology tends to go increasingly farther back in the child's evolution in order to understand the earliest beginnings of the psyche.

Her essay of capital importance, "Notes on some schizoid mechanisms" (Klein, 1946), appears in 1946. Up till then, Melanie Klein, all the while speaking of a paranoid–schizoid position, had in fact only gone into the "paranoid" side and neglected the "schizoid" side. Here again, the approach is subject to the desire to move still farther back in evolution. She sees in it the traces of all the initial psychotic fixations resulting from the first object relations which existed from the beginnings of life. She lays great emphasis on this, the initial tie, and describes the processes of splitting bringing out fragmentations of the ego. Splitting is at once internal and external. Splitting, denial, and omnipotence play a role comparable to that of repression in later stages implicated in neurosis. Oral fixation and the effects of the destructive drives converge. The projections have taken place *within* the mother (and not only *onto*).

At this point *projective identification* (projection of hatred against parts of the very person, directed against the mother; identification with the projected parts) is described. The expulsion also concerns the good parts, with as a consequence the fear of having lost the capacity to love despite the idealisation. The ego may experience the feeling that it has neither life nor autonomy. Violent splitting and excessive projection colour the persecutory tonality of the object. Melanie Klein insists— this is rare enough in her writings to be pointed out—on the *narcissistic nature* which derives from the infantile introjective and projective processes since the object causes only a part of the subject to be reflected. A feeling of artificiality emanates from them. Excessive narcissism impedes the elaboration of the paranoid–schizoid position towards the depressive position.

Thus, if the depressive position helps in understanding the psychogenesis of manic-depressive states, the study of schizoid mechanisms sheds light on schizophrenic states. Here again, Melanie Klein seeks to theorise what Freud left uncultivated or had only insufficiently developed.

Melanie Klein prompted dazzling interest in the British Psychoanalytical Society. Among those who joined her ranks are Joan Riviere, Susan Isaacs, Hanna Segal, John Sutherland, Paula Heimann (who subsequently distanced herself from her), and Herbert Rosenfeld. It isn't a question of drawing up a list of the members of the Kleinian school. Due to their interest in the psychoses in which Kleinian ideas were established, all these writers became representatives of the classic Kleinian school. Bion, emerging from this line, would soon distinguish himself through the originality of his own contributions.

Rosenfeld was doubtless the finest clinician of the Kleinian group. His reputation grew as a specialist of psychotic states. One of his most original contributions concerns narcissistic states. The Kleinian tendency to place first and foremost the accent on object relations brought about the neglect of narcissistic pathology. Rosenfeld described a destructive narcissism which, as I myself later suggested, is but one of the expressions of the death drive. He likewise delved deeper into projective identification and depersonalisation and confusional states. He clarified the notion of the psychosis of transference. Drug addiction and alcoholism further formed the object of his studies.

What may be said at the end of this brief review of Melanie Klein's ideas? If they aroused a great deal of enthusiasm and fervour, they also gave rise to radical objections and criticisms. Without going back to Edward Glover (1945), we will mention several of them:

1) The very dominant accent placed on the role of the destructive drives does not extend Freudian theory so much as denature it. For Freud, intrication and disintrication with the libido of the love and life drives were what mattered. Here, no equilibrium is respected; the field is filled entirely by the destructive drives.

2) For a great many analysts, Kleinians ignore the notion of the unconscious since they merely express the consciously perceived effects of destructiveness in the language of their own theory.

3) The exaggerated insistence on early states leads to a theory in which what is prior always explains what is later while endlessly pressing to move back the fixation points to orality, and even earlier.

4) External reality plays no role in and of itself. It depends exclusively on the acceptance of internal reality. This will be the object of Winnicott's dissension.

5) The Oedipus complex disappears since it cannot be reduced to what Melanie Klein says about it, and the father is something other than his representation as "penis of the father in the belly of the mother".

6) There exists an early superego prior to the Oedipus complex, a point contested by Freud himself.

7) The ego is reduced to its primitive mechanisms. Splitting, as Freud sees it disappears in favour of a Kleinian interpretation of this concept; it essentially separates the subjective aspects belonging to the bad object from those related to the good object.

8) Object relations are present from the very beginning. The evolution of the relations between ego and object hardly play any role.

9) Kleinians only read, cite, and take into account what other Kleinians write. Their essays' bibliographies express caricatural sectarianism.

Progress will not alter this state of things, which itself will be resolved by a virtual schism set into motion by Bion's thought. Open opposition to Klein's ideas further comes to light in Winnicott's writings.

Rereading Melanie Klein today, we see the analytic community divided between an admiration of her new vision, which has no misgivings about pushing the hypothesis of the death drive to a level from which even Freud would have backed off, and those who resist this infernal, apocalyptic vision that is difficult to accept in relation to what experience with children teaches us, which seems, for Klein, to have drowned its love libido in the blood bath of the destructive drives. There's no doubt that future Kleinians will be themselves tempted to pull back from this extremist design, which arouses a great many reservations. Alternate formulations will appear within the Kleinian movement in Bion's writings or with her fellow travellers, such as Winnicott.

Anyone who has been directly involved with Klein has observed her great rigour, her care before advancing an interpretation, and her knowledge of the infantile world. On the other hand, with time we have come to recognise that she was not a major theoretician and that judging her on these grounds was unnecessary. The fact remains that she decisively marked the evolution of psychoanalysis, even though she aroused virulent attacks and was long opposed. Within the International Psychoanalytical Association, she was left on the touchline before she became accepted. Even if she is bound to retain many critics, one cannot ignore who she was. But what is most interesting is that she made possible the spawning of works such as W. R. Bion's and D. W. Winnicott's. France, having a secret love affair with Jacques Lacan, will let her influence go by for quite some time. Was this a precocious intuition of a truth yet to be discovered or, rather, a tragic error?

2.3 W. R. Bion and the return to thinking

Devoting a specific section to Bion amounts not merely to wanting to dissociate him from Melanie Klein and her disciples—in other words, the classic Kleinian approach—but to recognising a distinct originality in his work defined, among other points, by a return to Freud's thinking and a resurgence of psychoanalytic concepts on thinking.

We won't examine in detail the elements of Bion's theory but settle for emphasising those related specifically to the death drive. One notion bridges Freudian theory and Kleinian theory. In *Beyond the Pleasure Principle*, Freud conceptualises the two essential mechanisms of binding and unbinding as characteristic of the functioning of Eros and the death drives. Now Bion in turn will make the concept of linking a pillar of his ideas. In his landmark essay, "Attacks on linking", he writes:

> I employ the term "link" because I wish to discuss the patient's relationship with a function rather than with the object that subserves a function; my concern isn't only with the breast or penis or verbal thought, but with their function of providing the link between two objects.
>
> (Bion, 1959, p. 147)

Two remarkable ideas appear in this definition. The first is the interest in a theory of functions. This is the first time that the expression "object relation" indicates what a relation is, namely, a function. The second idea integrates into the Kleinian concept into the idea that verbal thought forms the link between two objects. As a matter of fact, it is noteworthy that Bion is first and foremost interested in thinking and the repercussions of certain psychic functioning on it. Extending Klein's thinking, advanced in particular in "Notes on some schizoid mechanisms", he uses the mechanisms described by her on this occasion, including splitting, denial, omnipotence, evacuation, and expulsion in projective identification.

Bion sets great store by the last mechanism. He is led to describing "normal" projective identification in opposition to "excessive" projective identification in the same way that he postulates a virtually undetectable minute splitting. Bion's seminal thesis is summarised by a dilemma: evacuating frustration or modifying it. As in Freud, evacuation results in the accumulation of unpleasant tensions which impede the functioning of thinking. In the psychotic, frustration is not only linked to isolated libidinal satisfaction. The existence of the analyst as object embodies basic frustration with a desire to reject anything that comes from him or her; that is, to destroy the analyst-object and get rid of the fragments originating in the destruction, by all available means. Hatred is reinforced by the murderous attacks against what links the couple, against the couple itself, and against the object engendered by the couple. The role of the object is clarified here. Its challenge is to anticipate the threat and to experience the fear of the child, in whom was awakened the fear of dying. What is at stake is the receptivity to the child's projective identifications through the mother's *capacity for reverie*, which contributes to constructing in the child the alpha-function, a function which makes possible transforming raw sense impressions into material suitable for elaboration by the dream, myth, hallucination, and passion.

It is not only the preponderance of the destructive drives that is implicated but also the infiltration of the love drives by those which englobe at once inner and outer reality. They arouse a terror of imminent annihilation and implement premature and hurried development of precarious object relations constituted by a thin psychic stratum—that is, having no capacity for absorbing psychic processes.

One must count on the transference in order to perceive all the effects that we have just described. Even the psychic functions whose formation necessitates de facto links, such as the dream, must be reinterpreted within the frame of the destructive predominance. More than stimulating the function of integration, they are in fact used for evacuation. Bion concludes with a theory of thinking and non-thinking, a theory which cruelly points to the shortcomings of Kleinian thought.

Bion's great originality is the invention, alongside the Love (L) and Hate (H) factors, of a third fundamental category, Knowledge (K). Is this without equivalence in Freudian thought? May we not see in it an analogue of the function of binding, leading up to the pleasure principle, to which Freud is brought at the close of *Beyond the Pleasure Principle*?

But Bion's thinking is more complex still. He differentiates between Knowledge (K) and minus Knowledge (–K). The latter is underpinned by an omnipotence in which not knowing is more favourable than knowing. This, then, is what brings Bion and Freud together, the theoretician of masochism and the negative therapeutic reaction. Bion formulates the hypothesis that destructive attacks bring about evacuating an initial frustration. But should this frustration repeat itself, Bion postulates that the entire psyche is evacuated as a reaction to this repetition extending across the field of destruction.

With Bion, the death drive isn't explicitly mentioned but it becomes more imaginable, more acceptable and—I dare say—more thinkable. For such is the veritable stake of the drives of destruction: making the psyche unthinkable; seeing to it that it cannot bear thinking and that the very notion of causality is destroyed. "The model I propose for this development [hypertrophic development of the apparatus of projective identification] is a psyche that operates on the principle that evacuation of a bad breast is synonymous with obtaining sustenance from a good breast" (Bion, 1962, p. 155). This is a death-yielding equivalence which even leads, in some instances, to preferring ignorance through evacuation to the concern for understanding, the latter of which is the grounds for pleasure and the factor needed for growth. If the worst comes to the worst, it may sometimes feel best to evacuate the tension of life and prefer the reduction of death to zero.

2.4 D. W. Winnicott: the environment–individual pair

Where should we place Winnicott? When he went to New York to give a talk there in 1969, he was introduced and thought of as a Kleinian! This must have caught him by surprise since he had long seen the Kleinians as contentious. And, I might add, even today since in our own time he is the main target of the attacks of the Kleinians. Not that he ever denied the profound influence that Melanie Klein had on his thinking, but he was also mindful to emphasise where he disagreed with her. In addition, we could say that the Winnicottian turning point, towards the 1950s, was in our view just as paramount as that which marked the arrival of Melanie Klein onto the psychoanalytic scene around 1930.

But it's not merely in relation to Klein that there was dissent. It often happened that Winnicott put Freud and Klein in the same category in order to make his disagreement with them heard. One could say that the same argument which brings him into conflict with them is the reproach of exclusively taking interest in the inner world and neglecting the role of the environment, that is, the maternal "pathology", as if whether having a normal, neurotic, depressive, or psychotic mother made no difference. It's not a matter of taking into consideration a direct pathogenic role, but of asking how the traits characteristic of maternal behaviour are instrumental in organising the psychic personality of the child.

Winnicott's oeuvre is considerable and there is no question of summarising it here. On the other hand, Winnicott stated his view on the death drive very explicitly and so we may recall his arguments concerning it.

Winnicott takes a nuanced view concerning the role of destructiveness (there is no question for him of the death drive). He admits

its considerable influence, which he brings to the fore, just as Melanie Klein had earlier. We know that Winnicott has been counted among the partisans of object relations. In fact, it can be shown (Davis & Wallbridge, 1981) that this association was more moderate than one wished to say. Winnicott doesn't believe in the existence of the object at the beginning of life. *Human Nature* (Winnicott, 1988), an unfinished work, makes it possible to clarify his ideas on this point.

As a matter of fact, Winnicott doesn't believe it possible to think of the beginnings of life with respect to a distinct individual and object. For him, at the beginning, the individual self that is capable of separating ME from not-ME does not yet exist. In this state of primal non-differentiation there exists but a confused magma and infant observation—the field that is supposed to describe what characterises the baby—does not permit us to imagine, through the baby's eyes, "a stage at which there is a place to see from" (Winnicott, 1988, p. 131). It would be more convincing to envision an "environment–individual unit" at the earliest beginnings of psychic life. It would be even more acceptable to associate the being of the environment–individual pair to non-being as regards the first forms of this unity. A being would be born out of it in the wake of the exchanges between the two elements of the pair. However, this new emerging being only acquires the possibility of looming out of non-being because we need to recognise in the object an important activity, by way of the care it gives, without which we have no way of identifying in which form it exists when we hypothetically place ourselves in place of the baby. The baby, at this stage, has no consciousness of the environment or care given to him or her as such. The essential concern of the first stages is to ensure the continuity between intrauterine life and life outside, just as between the different aspects of psychic life. When the first steps unfold in a satisfying way, they prevent the reaction of impingement which leads to a premature and thus handicapping, parasitic consciousness of the object. The situation which Winnicott presents, in normalcy, promotes the development of autonomy and creativity already at work affecting the genesis of the object.

Of all the constructs that I am familiar with concerning the birth of the object at the beginnings of psychic life, Winnicott's seems to me the most convincing and, I should add, the only convincing one. It takes into account the links existing in reality but about which children can have no clear consciousness. The child experiences them as a feeling of totality—yet still dual—without any conscience of the fields making up the duality.

Faced with such a situation, the error consists in presenting them as either distinct rubrics (the viewpoint of the outsider) or the development of one of the two polarities, or even in retaining only the action of one of the two polarities, for instance, the object. Whence the ambiguity of the term "object relation". Relation between whom and whom? Relation of the object to whom? This is linguistic carelessness which in fact shrouds slipshod thinking.

Admittedly, Winnicott's theorising is hypothetical. But this speculation is more eloquent than the end result of a great many supposed truths marked by the blindness of an observer suffering from psychic rigidity. Winnicott pursues and suggests that this state born of the environment–individual pair, having no consciousness of an object whatsoever, corresponds to a state of "essential aloneness" which in all likelihood is related to what Freud calls primary narcissism. This may reappear in some regressions. Winnicott sees in it an equivalent to what Freud attributes to the functioning associated with the death drive.

Gaining access to this primitive form is scarcely simple. It is overlaid by the development of subsequent object relations (does it then concern what corresponds in Freud to "primary repression"?). Winnicott specifies that he then imagines "a peaceful state of unaliveness that can be peacefully reached by an extreme of regression" (Winnicott, 1988, p. 132). The proposed approximation with the death drive rests on the qualification of this state as "*before aliveness*" (Winnicott, 1988, p. 132; emphasis in the original).

To my knowledge, Winnicott never returns to this development in his published work. I find this a pity. But let's discuss his argument against Freud's ideas. One finds at the origin, just as in Freud, a state comparable to primary narcissism. Nothing other than this remark would suffice to differentiate Winnicott from the partisans, beginning with Michael Balint, of object relations for whom *primary narcissism does not exist*. Thus, Winnicott is not an "absolute" relationalist. The originality of the Winnicottian position is to affirm that the object exists (through the maternal care that it dispenses) and does not exist (since no *me* exists to recognise it). Essential aloneness? Are we so far from the withdrawal of the investments to the zero level? We must accept the ambiguity of the situations which may exist in reality without, however, there existing psychic organisations for recognising them. It is thus a matter of choosing between a situation perceptible from the outside but with no possibility of being perceived internally and a description which straightaway distinguishes the individual and the environment. This ambiguity is found in Winnicott with transitional objects, which are and are not the breast or the object.

We are wholly conscious of the importance of the Winnicottian mutation. At the same time, we observe the differences with Freud's hypotheses and their transformations in Melanie Klein and Bion. Contrary to what their detractors claim, psychoanalytic thinking undergoes constant transformation. It less displays rigidity than flexibility when speculation is defended in a convincing manner—not in a pseudo-realist way but as the product of an imagination free of bias.

2.5 Some French contributions
from Jacques Lacan to Claude Balier

French psychoanalysis over the past fifty years has been indisputably marked by Jacques Lacan, and so starting with him seems right. Yet Lacan never openly passed judgement on the death drive. In his early work the death drive is presented only as a philosophical mask, that is, death as Absolute Master. Should we attribute his use of it to the influence of Hegel during the period when the first part of Lacanian theory was being worked out? Without a doubt. In any case, afterwards Lacan no longer alludes to it in this guise. Is it possible to say for all that that the ideas overlying the notion disappear? I hold that the concept of jouissance may be associated with it in so far as jouissance indirectly relates its forms to the death drive. This, in particular, is jouissance in the sense of horror, that which the serious forms of perversion express—whether destructive or related to psychosis. Nevertheless, the theory of the death drive remains in abeyance.

Along the lines of Lacan, Jean Laplanche resolutely speaks out against the Freudian theory of the death drive. To Freud's final drive theory opposing death drives and life drives, he prefers his own, which differentiates between death sex drives and life sex drives. The first are understandable in terms of chaos whereas the second have already undergone the preliminaries of organisation. Doesn't this amount to adopting a monist theory of the destructive or constructive libido? In our view, it is advisable to oppose chaos, the lot of the Freudian id, and nothingness, the tendency to annihilation (zero level) of inertia and Nirvana. For instance, the drive's inhibition isn't due to the establishment of chaos but rather to the extinction of any expression by the drive, which is even capable of affecting self-preservation (anorexia).

Turning to another frontier of clinical practice, Pierre Marty was earnest about Freud's ideas, all the while modifying them. The paradigm of destructiveness is certainly a notion which speaks to psychosomaticians, who at times observe a triumph of death not always explainable by the gravity of somatic disorders. But Marty prefers to speak of "counter-progressing disorganisations". Whatever the case, the psychosomaticians' descriptions make room for the concept of the death drive without straining the facts. We shall return to this point. It is worth pointing out that this only becomes meaningful when coupled with the concept of the life drive.

Returning to ordinary psychoanalytic clinical work, Jean-Claude Rolland's understanding is distinguished by its originality. Rolland never fails to make reference to Freud's essay on "A child is being beaten". The masochistic accumulation of the failures of the ego, the search for unconscious sanctions satisfying the need for self-punishment, and the multiplication of negative therapeutic reactions driving to the search for increasingly painful treatments attest, in his view, to the intensity of unconscious guilt which demands incessant punishments boiling down to the realisation of the fantasy of being beaten by the father. That the erotic libido in these cases cannot but be enacted because it lacks other ways by which it may seek being satisfied, so be it. But what becomes of eroticism when invoking the death drive? Should we look to the solution on the side of full-blown sadomasochism? I hardly think so since, at the very least, we ought to speak of deteriorated erotic libido. For Freud, we should recall, unconscious affect is without qualities. At the most, we may oppose states of great drive excitation and apathy resembling psychic death. Here it is rather a matter of a drive frenzy literally riveted onto its goal and bringing about depersonalisation. This is what the pathology of severe perversion shows. In these instances, it isn't the unconscious which is at work but the id possessing an erotic and destructive bipolarity.

We should also mention the work of Micheline Enriquez (1984). This bears on what she terms the "crossroads of hatred". She puts the accent on the hatred-suffering complex and turns her attention to paranoia, masochism, and apathy, and further underscores the elective affinities between paranoia and masochism. Apathy may be understood as an attempt at mastering psychic death.

The work of Claude Balier (1996, 2005) on psychoanalytic psychocriminology further needs to be discussed. His contributions upend our understanding of destructiveness. Balier began publishing the findings of his investigations into the sexual pathology of violent behaviour in 1966. His narratives give the shivers. Rape is understood as the effect of a compulsion, a constraining process. When it is preceded by psychic productions, they are the object of denial accompanied by disidentification. This is often accompanied by other forms of acting out, including suicide, self-mutilation, or raping a fellow inmate. Oneiric activity is often exclusively inhabited by the nightmare. "Fantasies" also emerge and include the fear of being raped oneself or the fantasy of raping another. Psychotic motifs come to light in dreams (infanticide by the subject's parents) or the feeling of imploding with unbearable suffering in the head.

Frequently encountered are profuse pregenital phobias poorly containing conversion hysteria, each possessing a "primitive" character indicating a threat of annihilation (*néantisation*) likened to night-time terrors. The sexual is in the service of violence (Bergeret, 1984). The problem of outer–inner boundaries is mentioned concerning the relationships between fantasy, perception, and hallucination. If a parental image is prevalent, it is the mother's, the primary object. In the inner world, the good is inaccessible while the bad is constantly intrusive (Donnet & Green, 1973). Acting out is an attempt at resolving by means of a discharging of the bad. Among the predominating affects are rage and violence. Negative hallucination (André Green) and the pictogram (Piera Aulagnier) are helpful in conceptualising the psyche. In addition, the ego's frontiers are poorly established, incriminating the inside/outside (inner/outer) boundary and inside/inside boundary (between conscious, preconscious, and unconscious). The predominating defences are denial and splitting. Conflict and the act are radically split. In fact, the ego's very foundations are frail: there exists the fear of breakdown which is accompanied by a "primary three-way confusion". This is perhaps explained by the fact that the rapist-to-be has often been raped himself during childhood. Narcissistic depression is frequently encountered at the basis of the psyche. Murder is often the result of a particular omnipotence, that of a grandiose ego; hatred is preponderant, just as sadism, passivation (forced passivity), and the fear of loving share parts of the clinical picture. Incest is the model of perversion par excellence.

Claude Balier undertakes a convincing metapsychological construction which doesn't directly put the death drive into play. The whole of the psyche regresses: drive, narcissism, projection, abolition of the object dimension of the other as other. Within it one finds the raw expressions of the primal scene, the worry aroused by the parental imagos conveying a failure of introjecting of the phallus. These forms of perversion border on psychosis and comprise a threat of disobjectalisation with a violation of the sentiment of identity, a desire for ascendancy over the other and negative hallucination leading to a kind of abolishing of the subject. The threat of depersonalisation weighs on differing actings out. In such cases the work of binding lays bare its deficiencies.[43]

Balier returns to all these problems some years later in a collective work with his collaborators (Balier, 2005, p. 146). The parental imagoes are incriminated: "Is it a matter of a paternal figure?" The answer: "The father being admired and inaccessible, the figure who originates in him is a *representation having a direct affiliation with the ideal ego*, whence the idea that it is preferable to say, the 'non-mother'" (Claude Le Guen). The second remark is the following: as strong as the impression is of a pathology having an intersubjective origin, it nonetheless establishes a connection between two intrapsychic organisations.

The role of sociogenesis in criminality which takes over from psychogenesis bears mentioning. In conclusion, we should emphasise that what is most difficult in relationships with such subjects is to keep reminding ourselves that they have the right on the part of their therapists to the same respect as the rest of humankind.

---

[43] The work of Rosine Jozef Perelberg and her research group (P. Fonagy, M. Target, D. Campbell, and others) has shed much light on the problems of clinical work on violence in psychoanalysis. It should be noted that these writers do not raise the question of the death drive. Cf. Perelberg (1999).

2.6 Pierre Marty's psychosomatics

Among the pathologies now called somatoses (by analogy with the psychoses), some pose novel problems. Psychosomatic incidences were identified long ago, going back at least to the nineteenth century. A person who is allergic to violets triggers an asthma attack when seeing a bouquet of artificial flowers. Instances abound in which a critical condition is set into motion by the effects of simulation. What is known as psychosomatic medicine was often founded on an aetiology of "shocks" or traumas, a notion which with time has become outmoded. The role of suggestion has similarly been highlighted by many writers. In analytic movements throughout the world, one always finds a doctor who describes clinical pictures based on a debatable pathogenesis, relating somatic symptom to psychic event. Thus, the patient suffering from hypertension was "hypertensive" while the ulcerous individual was "worried" (in French, "*se faisait de la bile*") and the nervous one had "nerves stronger than blood". This idea, whose roots are found in folk wisdom, did not go very far. When psychotherapy proved advisable in the fight against such states, what was most often recommended was supportive psychotherapy or, better yet, hypnosis (which has come back in vogue) and, nowadays, cognitive behavioural therapy. Short-term therapy and those with a quick effect were preferred. It was a matter ridding the psyche of useless congestion.

Throughout the world there exists a great diversity of schools in which well-known names have distinguished themselves, among them Franz Alexander, Helen Flanders Dunbar, Medard Boss, and others. In France, René Held and Michel Sapir in particular should be mentioned. In fact, despite the interest of many psychoanalysts, no truly specifically psychosomatic understanding was developed. With Pierre Marty, the founder of the Paris Psychosomatic School, a novel psychoanalytic understanding came to light. The school's influence gradually reached international circles and gained recognition, even if many psychoanalysts continued to manifest their disagreement with Marty's concepts.

We cannot cover all the areas in which psychoanalytic advances have made it possible to make progress, though they include back pain, headaches, allergies, ulcerative colitis, glaucoma, dermatosis, and so on. We will have to make do with mentioning certain ideas identified by

Pierre Marty and his colleagues, Michel Fain, Michel de M'Uzan, and Christian David (cf. Marty, M'Uzan, & David, 1963). Marty's theory was carried on after his death by Claude Smadja, Marilia Aisenstein, and Gérard Szwec; de M'Uzan developed his own concept. Together with de M'Uzan in 1962, Marty described "operational thinking", which since then has become "operational life" (Marty & M'Uzan, 1962). It was a matter—I'm summarising greatly—of describing the psyche of individuals imbued with abrasive pragmatism and managing little by little to wear away their psychic life of any vitality—of any desire—and to think, feel, and reason in a way exempting them from any recourse to fantasy. Such mental behaviour calls for several remarks:

1) The reference to *mental functioning*—a specifically French notion and little used elsewhere—in which is observed the lack of fluidity and vitality of the psyche, which doesn't take into account the psychic equilibrium between differing modalities including language, oneiric activity, fantasies, affects, enactments, and somatisation. And in which it is noted that the formations stemming from character (character and behaviour neuroses) play a prevalent role. We typically compare the neurotic's mental functioning to the psychotic's. Henceforth we must consider comparing it to the psychosomatic patient's.

2) *Irregularity of the preconscious*: the role of the preconscious which, as we know, is the part of the unconscious liable to becoming conscious, was recognised in contemporary psychoanalysis as increasingly important for psychic equilibrium. According to Marty, the "thickness" of the preconscious must be taken into consideration as a buffer zone between the unconscious and the conscious. Marty uses the expression "foliage" of the preconscious, imagining a superposition of layers in which psychic working-through occurs. However, according to Marty's theory, the preconscious records but does not emit, that is to say that these messages are not received at the level of the conscious psyche.

3) In fact, this observation goes hand in hand with such patients' *poverty of fantasy life*. It has been remarked that at times fantasy life, far from being absent, was not, on the whole, integrated into psychic life, as if it took place outside it.

4) *Operational functioning* completes this picture in which is seen a mechanising of the psyche which scarcely associates at all. The speech of these patients is stereotypical; it isn't revitalised by associative psychic life. They're born and die treading water, buried by a "that's all" which prohibits any development and in consequence impoverishes the deductions that one might draw from the relationships between associations.

It is necessary, however, to differentiate patients who exhibit but a few psychosomatic traits from those having a genuine psychosomatic profile. Among the defences, which are typical of them, are described *self-calming* behaviours, which in these cases replace autoeroticism and play less a role of substitutive satisfying than extinguishing through exhaustion.

We may add to this broad configuration some grievous signs:

1) The clinical picture of *essential depression*, with neither object loss nor significant psychic conflict, constituted by atony and a decrease in psychic vitality and diminished energy, which suggests predictable psychic death.
2) The extension of progressive *operational life* marked by the dullness and colourless character of the psyche which appears flattened and listless.
3) The tending towards a *progressive disorganisation* in which the psychic processes and the somatic processes reflect what Marty calls "counter-evolutive disorganisations" indicative of an ascendancy by the destructive drives.

What should we think of the death drive in these occurrences in which the vital mechanisms appear neutralised? Without overindulging in the language of vitalism, this means that since psychic conflicts cannot be worked through, the "noise of life" is deafened. Silence, the background on which, according to Freud, the death drives act, feeds the psyche with disorganising unbinding. It happens that the clinical pictures evolve, despite appropriate treatment, towards a state of physical worsening which may lead to death.

Such are the characteristics we are reminded of in cases of psycho-somatic pathology. These ideas have stimulated a great deal of interest in psychoanalytic circles in France and other countries and have made it possible to spread the ideas of the psychoanalysts of the Paris School. So far as I know, the polemics have not come to a halt. In a significant way, the design of the French Psychosomatic School can, by and large, be opposed to that of Kleinian and English-speaking writers.

We see that this theorising considers the difference between the ideas of the Paris School and the opposing theory, which is based on conversion (Valabrega, 1980), with great seriousness. Nonetheless, whereas the idea of generalised conversion has hardly been confirmed, psychosomatics has taken on ever more adepts.

The idea of a face-off between psychosis and somatosis is increasingly necessary. The ideas advanced these last years on the comparison between Lacanian foreclusion and operational life have given birth to some interesting discussions. Notions such as negative hallucination further find an application, which isn't unrelated to Peter Sifneos' alexithymia (Sifneos, 1975).[44] In short, the work of the negative sees a new field of exploration open up.

Lastly, these cases call for important technical modifications. They require finding alternative solutions to classic psychoanalytic treatment, including face-to-face, less-frequent sessions, and the implementing of a "psychoanalytic conversation" (Roussillon, 2005) due to the impossibility of establishing a classic setting. Psychosomatic pathologies increasingly belong to the research fields of psychoanalytic therapeutics; since they comply poorly with the model of neurosis, which is the standard for classic psychoanalytic treatment, they by and large constitute what psychosomaticians call neuroses presenting insufficient mentalisation.

2.7 Disruption of self-preservation

If we speak of the death drive while pushing its sought-after aim to an extreme, we find that the goal of such force is to succeed in killing the individual. Yet few examples of this kind are advanced in support

---

[44] Alexithymia is the impossibility of reading one's own affects and thus verbalising them.

of the thesis. Adult psychosomatics presents us with clinical pictures which may evolve towards death through essential disorganisation. But these cases, staggering though they are, are far from being the only ones which lead patients to die. Without claiming to be exhaustive, we would like to add to this ensemble the cases of disruption of self-preservation. We will separate them into two categories, eating disorders and drug addictions.

The first are in part due to the massive inhibiting of appetite, the cradle of self-preservation. Inhibition holds but a limited place in Freud's work. Naturally we recall *Inhibitions, Symptoms and Anxiety* (1926). Hardly forty pages introduce the subject in what will be Freud's key work on anxiety. This is quite insufficient but it's better than nothing. Without supposing that inhibition and symptom rule each other out, they may be brought into relation. Freud then settles for indicating the four functions where he identifies inhibition: the sexual function, feeding, locomotion, and professional work. A difference is straightaway blindingly obvious. One can survive without sexuality and without moving or working, but not without eating. A hunger strike, pursued to its conclusion, ends with the striker's death. Everything thus predisposes the feeding inhibition to a particularly serious fate. Freud very often used the aphorism that maintains that hunger and sex dominate the world, yet he did not devote any particular study to anorexia.

The taking of food (and putting on weight) is a source of anxiety for the anorexic. Bulimia also comes under a disruption of the mechanism of self-preservation but without bringing about the same consequences, although chronic, incurable obesity has its effects on health. In such cases, vomiting presents itself as a partial solution. So it is among anorexics who also force themselves to vomit after a meal. "I'm going Roman," said the father of one of my patients, himself particularly preoccupied by his weight and shape and a great lover of thin women having a "model's waist".

Freud calls these states "restrictions of an ego-function" (1926, p. 89). He attributes their cause to self-punishment due to the sexualisation of the function either out of caution or the impoverishing of energy. It seems that this pathology—anorexia, above all—has met with robust growth, judging by the number of studies devoted to it (Brusset, 1977; Combe, 2002; Jeammet, 2004). We cannot cite in any detail these writers' findings and hypotheses since they are all complex, on a par moreover with the subject itself. We will only point out in passing that bygone coercive methods have abided with the psychotherapeutic relationship taking precedence, psychotherapy being well adapted to this pathology which is hypersensitive to any and all rejection, frustration, and incomprehension. Colette Combe defends a truly original psychosomatic position when she emphasises the constancy of a disturbance of hormonal equilibrium as one of the most discrete signs attesting to anorexia in the process of constitution.

It is satisfying to observe frequent recovery today. We might emphasise that therapy shows the consistency of a poor acceptance of feminine sexuality (phobia of the transformation of a juvenile body into a body endowed with "lures", that is, breasts, stomach, and buttocks). The subject seeks to dissimulate these marks of sexual difference so far as possible. We may observe a refusal of sex, a refusal of the relation with the sexual other, and pregenital conflicts with the maternal image leading in the end to a refusal of life. Dying from anorexia is a distinct possibility.

Bulimia, which is frequent without anorexia and potentially coexists with an entirely healthy appetite, manifests itself intermittently. When a crisis occurs, the complete contents of the refrigerator are consumed, in disorder, followed or not by vomiting. Moreover, measures against possible obesity are implemented, including vomiting, laxatives to flatten the stomach, strenuous gymnastics, exhausting sport, and so on. In my experience, bulimia organises itself on the basis of an aggressive, destructive reaction with regard to a close relation, such as a mother or sister. The subject is astonished by the interpretations suggested by the analyst since a great deal of time is necessary before becoming conscious of the truly destructive hostility dedicated to a loved one about whom, moreover, he or she is dependent, or was so during childhood.

Putting drug addiction, which is also appearing with greater frequency due to the easier accessibility of toxic substances, into the same section heading might seem debatable. Without claiming any expertise in the subject, I would empirically distinguish "drugs which kill quickly" from those whose more benign and slower action only signals their harmful effects belatedly without being life-threatening. It will be understood that I am making a distinction between heroin and everything else, even if there exist other very dangerous drugs with which their consumers are playing at cheating death.

We needn't remind ourselves of the gravity of the antisocial behaviour of subjects dying for a fix. It is less a question of stigmatising behaviour than emphasising that lack is a factor in a genuine delirium for procuring the drug, if necessary, even by robbing mother and father. Here again, the analyst requires a great deal of experience if he or she is to know how to resist the sabotage and initiatives of despondency and despair faced with relapses before there might emerge a possible opening long afterwards. But let's state clearly that overdose is unwitting suicide. Quite a few family members and friends have in view consoling themselves by differentiating an overdose from a suicide attempt. The distinction is vain, a superficial explanation that doesn't mask the all-too-painful wounds for the entourage of an especially desperate act.

One sees in all these cases that the death drive is not merely a metaphorical catchphrase. It must be taken literally. But the traders in death who deal in drugs are utterly unconcerned. As one of them said while trying to make a journalist feel guilty, "Everybody's got to make a living."

2.8 Unity and diversity of depression

Given that in 1923 Freud designates melancholia as "a pure culture of the death drive" (1923, p. 53), it would be paradoxical not to give it a separate study. Freud's work in 1915, "Mourning and melancholia" (1917), is surely one of his most accomplished studies. From about 1909, he discussed it—mainly in letters—with Karl Abraham, to whom we owe some of the most poignant intuitions on the subject, most particularly on oral fixation. Yet, as Freud made his disciple acknowledge, melancholia is above all a topographical problem. We should understand by this that the division of the ego, between one part identified with the object so as to replace its loss and another which persists in obeying its traditional functions, ushers in a new mechanism in Freudian psychopathology. The other components of melancholia (regression to an oral stage, cannibalistic fixation, predominance of hate), all the while maintaining their importance, nevertheless fall behind the topographical question. In fact, imagining that the ego may split so that one of its parts may take the lost object's place is a capital intuition and readily pinpoints the narcissistic regression which concerns the ego. Whence the ambiguity of suicide. Who is killed? Oneself, or part of the other which finds itself replaced in its loss by a part of the ego? Deciding isn't always easy. This gives us an indication of the complexity of how the death drive operates.

Discussion has long concerned the distinctiveness or range of depressive forms. It is true that we are familiar with diverse forms of depression, including *reactional*, consecutive to an event experienced as traumatic; *seasonal*, due to the lack of light in cold weather; *involution*, caused by the effects of the aging brain; the *essential depressions* of the psychosomatoses; and so on. But, in practice, in ordinary situations, the problem is how to distinguish between *melancholia*—monopolar or bipolar psychosis—and *neurotic depression*.

We should state straight away that a depressive reaction is rarely lacking in the course of the analytic cure. When broaching the critical and difficult problems of transference, it isn't unusual to observe take hold a regressive period conveying all the aspects of depression. Whether a realisation of the importance of unconscious guilt or narcissistic devaluing, of romantic or professional failure, of the feeling of disappointing the analyst and never being able to answer what one believes to be his or her expectations, the motives converge towards the formation of a clinical picture in which predominate pessimism, discouragement, apathy, resignation, and withdrawal. These episodes, with or without analysis, may be repeated, indeed, they may possibly lead to suicide attempts, however less frequently than in the course of melancholic states. They may be short-lived and disappear with or without medication or more often after taking anti-depressants ranging from the weakest to the strongest. Anti-depressant treatment may be used and is often effective. However, it gives patients the impression of being "outside themselves", as if they were faintly concerned by the changes taking place within. The idea of not having to go and search beyond the recapturing of serotonin is the fruit of pharmaco-mechanistic psychiatric thinking which often encourages a denial of psychic activity. Some psychiatrists themselves condemn it. Henceforth, in the eyes of general practitioners, banal mourning, romantic disappointment, or a marital or professional problem warrant the prescription of anti-depressants.

Why suffer to no purpose, making a point to ignore—this is the result of the camouflaged manic defence—that suffering is part of life? This "chemical hedonism", it must be said, is dehumanising. It even happens that some animals may find themselves sad.

I have described a form of depression that I called the "dead mother". This is a matter, contrary to what the term might appear to indicate, of a living mother's depression but having, subsequent to an event unknown to her child, lost the lust for life, that is, the will to look after the child in a living way with the part of joy which normally goes hand in hand with maternal care. I will not go back to a detailed description, to which the interested reader may turn (Green, 1980). This syndrome is often enough detected in the transference, and it well puts the analyst to the test. Many others have since confirmed this clinical structure.

In all likelihood, other traditionally unacknowledged clinical forms will be found. What is essential is handling the plurality presented by the range of depressions in order to bring out the innermost unity of the depressive fixations and defences. From essential depression, in principle a-conflictual—a depression in the atmospheric sense of the term—to involutional depression ascribable, assuming there is no error, to a brain state, every shade comprising the depressive array has its place. From severe, stubborn, and recurring melancholic depressions often requiring a recourse to electroconvulsive therapy after medication fails, to the profoundly organised "simple" affective conflict, entailing a threat, or a reality, of loss of love on the part of the object, great are the opportunities and circumstances which may foster the spawning of depression.

Should the death drive be incriminated in each and every case? This we cannot affirm, save when the velleities or serious threats of suicide arise. And even then, the matter is open to discussion. Notwithstanding, the more we are dealing with "closed-off" narcissism that is impenetrable to any relationship with the other and which, as in melancholia, is the bearer of genuine delirium, the more the intervening of the self-destructive drives appears founded. Life's diversity sees to providing an *après-coup* understanding of the reasons for the depressive attack and the causes assessed in accordance with the narcissistic coefficient, the early ripening of the fixations, and the intensity of unconscious hate.

2.9 Pathology and normality of suicide(s)

Oddly, suicide is not much of an issue in Freud's conceptualising of the death drive. Yet it is a major concern for psychoanalysts when melancholia arises. And as I mentioned above, in 1923 Freud rightly described melancholia as "a pure culture of the death drive" (1923, p. 53). Perhaps he doesn't discuss suicide because it isn't organically or exclusively tied to the death drive and it involves many complex motivations, such as killing someone else by taking one's own life. But the question remains puzzling.

Whatever the case, it is also the analyst's main preoccupation during especially challenging periods in the course of the cure. Whatever the starting point of the pathology which may lead to suicide, the suicidal juncture is specifically that of a massive turnaround of destruction directed against the ego. This moment may be observed in the most varied structures. Theatrical hysteria can be of surprise when acted out, but so too, may character neuroses, borderline states, and some psychoses other than melancholia (paranoia). We are consciously in the presence of a spectrum of states ranging from the desire to put an end to suffering that has become intolerable to the extreme despair which characterises melancholia. But we may also observe an impulsive movement crop up, an overwhelming fit which nothing makes possible to predict and which is contemporaneous with the feeling that the analyst may have about the subject who has retreated into an impasse from which he or she doesn't know how to get out of other than by saying "no" to life by means of a leap implying the desire to be done away with it. We see that the forces of destruction cannot be solely invoked, even though at the moment the subject acts out they are drawn on to the full.

Aggression is directed against the other before being directed against the subject him- or herself. Thus the desire to harm the parents, often enough the father in order to reproach him for his passivity and lack of interest, is every so often at the forefront. But also faulted is the mother, the object of the earliest, oral fixations. This harming is more often sensed by the entourage than the subject before committing suicide, who clings less to the idea of putting an end to their life than to their suffering and perhaps denies any aggressive intent towards the parents. The transference however shows this perfectly, but this intent remains opaque to the subject and is denied when brought up by others. These desires are unconscious. They are not satisfied with expressing an aggressive drive but bid to harm the ego. This is to say that narcissism is struck, whence a feeling of insufficiency, failure, depreciation, and, above all, the loss of hope of seeing the situation change.

I myself have defended (Green, 1994) the idea that suicide may be caused by the desire to bring an end, not to actual life properly speaking, but to a future which will only get worse. Withdrawing from life means stopping the unsurmountable advance of pain; giving oneself over to this definitive self-demise in order not to feel still more one's own infirmity each and every day. We may further identify the particularly difficult-to-bear feeling of being but the shadow of oneself and presenting oneself as a spectacle for the other, intensifying still more a deterioration even more difficult to experience as it is produced among subjects with sensitive and projective narcissism. We should recall here Freud's very pertinent remark in "Mourning and melancholia" emphasising the contrast between a strong object fixation and a weak investment.

The fixation, we know, is oral-aggressive, while the weakness of the investment refers to the way by which it may be withdrawn in the event of disappointment in the object. It bears repeating that in suicidal depression it is less a matter of frustration than disappointment—disappointment in the object, to be sure, from which much is expected and doubtless unrealistically, but above all disappointment bearing on the subject's own self-esteem. We see that our descriptions are situated in proximity with melancholia, when the desire to be no longer prevails by means of an act bolstered with reproaches addressed to the other, as much as to oneself. To the other in neurotic depressions, to the self in melancholia. The desire for self-punishment is patent but also that of affecting others by means of this very act. "Look what you've done to me. You weren't able to breath the love of life or hope for the future or self-esteem into me like you did with the others." In such a case there exists a denial of the recognition of the love that the others have for the subject. This is a projection onto the others of one's incapacity to love.

Dwelling on this question is pointless since no one knows, can know, what death is—just as speculations on life after death, seeking to make up for the anxiety of an unknowable emptiness, prove. But for the suicidal individual at least as much for the others, death is conceived as peace for the soul at long last achieved. Such a thought is solace for life's torments, for the feeling of not being loved and never being capable of being loved. It even happens that some successful attempts cause others to think in a similar way about the person who has committed suicide and those who pass away after a painful, incurable illness; that is, they suffer no longer. Their suffering cannot be minimised, even in cases in which it isn't a matter of melancholia. In some forms of psychosis, this may be the feeling of being indefinitely overwhelmed, interfered with, and appropriated by an object which strips one's identity and wounds by its very existence, and which makes life hateful.

Sometimes suicide is supposed to provide proof that one is so little attached to life that one is prepared to leave it at any time. Thus, Kirillov tears himself away from the Dostoyevskian universe and offers his life up to anyone who asks him for it as proof that God does not exist. This metaphor perhaps underpins the desire to prove that the universe is absurd, that it has no meaning, and thus that suicide is not an offence to God—since there isn't any. This grants Him more importance than consenting to such self-sacrifice.

Sometimes, and even more frequently, the opposite situation is observed. In many religions, loving God means suffering for Him. Among the first members of the sects predating Christianity, the followers were proud to suffer and even sacrifice their life for the Master of justice. There is no need to go back so far in History, which is replete with sacrificial deaths.

At the time I was writing this work, someone who was familiar with my study asked me if I would go into the theme of suicide bombers, who are incorrectly called kamikazes.[45] I shall plead ignorance: I have never met such men and women neither near nor far. Nevertheless, this doesn't suffice to putting a stop to thinking about the matter. It seems to me that suicide bombers represent, for nations at war and not equipped with sophisticated technical means, something like a perfect weapon. Other than the fact that in paradise the hero who immolates himself is, in some cases, eagerly awaited by seventy virgins (seventy! enough to satisfy the most voracious appetites!) and that the family counts on

---

[45] Translator's note: Green is alluding to how the term "kamikaze" is used in France where, in addition to its historical meaning, it refers to contemporary suicide bombers.

financial compensation—the price for the heroic sacrifice—we have much to ponder. On the one hand, this is the negation of any individual desire—other than the individual who sacrifices him- or herself for the cause—which leads to an all-embracing identification with the arm used (the bomb), and on the other the hoped-for means of winning all at once. For how may one defeat someone who turns a loss into a win while ignoring the desire to spare his or her life?

In such cases, human loss is compensated by a benefit for the divinity. In *The Iliad* each soldier bitterly defended his skin. The gods intervened in the game by deflecting the arrows against the enemy and diverting the path of the spear that was supposed to strike them. For suicide bombers, none of these surprises needs to occur. No god is called on to guide the destruction against oneself—and against a few others. This reversal of self-preservation suggests self-destruction, but the suicide bomber would answer back that this is simply the surest means of killing the other. Is this suicide? You can't be serious! More likely, it is martyrdom!

I won't go into the sociological aspects of suicide, which are becoming quite familiar and which bring a different viewpoint to the question. In brief, speaking of suicide means accepting and adopting positions spanning the strictest intimacy related to the defeat of the desire to live to still more remote ones which merely take into consideration the phenomenon from the viewpoint of the law of averages and are preoccupied with comparing different populations. Durkheim (1897), in his sociological study on suicide, doesn't help us *subjectively* understand what it is about. If psychoanalysis can, its arguments do not always succeed in curbing the desire to cease living. Does it prevent the death of "heroic" drug addicts or Formula 1 racing-car drivers? The risk of death is part of the excitement of living. What else can one do? Play tarot on Saturday evenings? No thanks! In this case, each wakening is a resurrection, each victory a new birth.

I wish to make a final point. Suicide is a recurrent temptation. Some patients make five, ten, or twenty attempts before they accept living. They may even, despite being well-versed in lethal products and dosages, amaze themselves by waking up, despite having followed all the instructions which should have swept them off to the hereafter. They surprise themselves in having to concede that, perhaps, they didn't want to die as much as they'd believed.

One question dividing researchers is if all suicides are always patho-logical. Are there normal suicides, thought of as clear-headed gestures? I cannot reply with certainty. All I know is that if I came down with a serious and incapacitating illness, constraining my physical and above all psychic means, I would like to be able to decide to leave the scene without being suspected of having committed a senseless act. It also happens that, suffering from infirmity, one loses consciousness of one's state (Alzheimer's) and lives on.

An act of this kind makes it possible to die in dignity, and so it is that Freud asked his physician, Max Schur, to help him take that step when the time came. No one considered blaming the misdeeds of the death drive. He believed that it was time to stop and asked for morphine to do its job in order to avoid pointless suffering. Max Schur gave it to him, which brought about a peaceful death. This is a destiny I envy.

2.10 Brief remarks on clinical practice

The theory of the death drive espoused by Freud with regard to the rep-etition compulsion construes psychic states observed during the cure, including neuroses, depressions, borderlines, and sometimes psychoses, in a new way. The two clinical fields that we have gone into, those com-ing under psycho-criminality and psychosomatics, are significantly dif-ferent. With psycho-criminality, the clinical picture is dominated by what Balier calls the "recourse to the act", namely, that the solution by the act appears as a constraint, without in such structures there being any hope of psychic working-through. Quite the opposite, with psycho-somatics, as somatisation seems to be the recourse required by the fail-ure of the psychic organisation, deficient at the level of the preconscious. In other words, this solution makes it necessary to distinguish between the "body traversed by the signifier" (Lacan), which may account for conversion, and somatosis and acting out in which *at the level of the symptom* no structuration by the signifier may be invoked.

This is an interesting symmetry. Everything happens as if the "men-tal thing" represented only a "psychisised"[46] portion of a broader whole.

---

[46] Translator's note: The admittedly barbaric adjective, "psychisised", has no prec-edent in English but is modeled on *psychisé*, which moreover is hardly more common

The verbosity is appreciated. The psyche is the psychised portion. In truth, if this psychisation seems tautological, it's because defining it is onerous. In a word, we may say that as it is focused by the drive, it is susceptible, by virtue of its representations, to evolve towards a form of relating with the Other. The Other exists explicitly and plays its role in the construction of symptoms and in the clinical picture. If this is easily illustrated by the clinical pictures of psycho-criminality, it is less readily applicable to psychosomatics. We have already underscored the role of somatosis in which an unsignified body is at work. We will add to this that the unconscious is put out of play; or rather outside the I?[47] Symptomatology short-circuits it and reaches psychic zones falling short of the pleasure principle.

The appearances of the death drive surface well beyond the pleasure principle in which death, the other's or one's own, is but very insufficiently curbed by a psyche "with gaping holes in it".

Such is the coherence of clinical thinking. There is no doubt as to the need to expect fresh progress on this parallel between external acting out and internal acting out (cf. Green, 1973).

Fermata

The impact of Freud's revolutionary text from 1920 continues to be felt by the analytic community after well more than half a century. What may be said about it? We could summarise the situation as such: "The words have been rejected; the matter, on the other hand, in general recognised." For, in fact, if we only rarely encounter the expression "death drive" in the writings of those who see themselves as heirs to

---

in French. Green further uses a related term, *psychisation*, sometimes found (like *somatisation*) in literature originating in the Paris Psychosomatic School. Claude Smadja, for example, writes: "We've seen that for Freud, while the body's work of psychisation is based on the equilibrium of the mechanisms of binding and unbinding within the affect-representation combination, for Green the body's work of psychisation is based more fundamentally and earlier on the formation of the primitive drive-object cell, that is, on the union of the body and the object world" (Smadja, 2011, p. 157).

[47] Translator's note: Green is making the most of the homonyms, *hors-jeu*, "out of play" or "out of the game", and *hors Je*, "outside the I", a pun also made by Lacan.

Freud's legacy, we surely observe, from Ferenczi up through our own time, that the central problem of psychoanalysis today is to be found precisely among the varied forms of destructiveness. Such consistency is telling. It is, moreover, problematic since it is achieved at the expense of the place of sexuality, which is constantly revised downwards to the advantage of various new concepts. In fact, after Freud and Ferenczi, with Melanie Klein a theoretical mutation modified the perspective of psychoanalysis. Thereafter, various writers have had to approve or more generally combat the Kleinian point of view as much if not more than Freudian theory. However, reflection on the death drive didn't end with the writers who came after Melanie Klein. Following the death of all the great figures of psychoanalysis whose differences we've made out and whose stances we've summarised, a new generation has appeared. For there can be no question of turning the page on the death drive without giving oneself the possibility of examining all the aspects of the Freudian concept once more. This is why our commentary doesn't finish with contemporary contributions but goes "back upstream"[48] towards the work of the discoverer of the death drive. As debatable as his ideas are, they are, in my view, those which are the most suggestive.

[48] Translator's note: *Retour amont*, "Back Upstream", is the title René Char gave to his 1966 collection of poems.

CHAPTER 3

The death drive in the social field: *Discomfort in Culture*

3.1 The death drive in culture

Reminding ourselves of the influence of Freud's training in biology on the theory that he developed is something we often appreciate. This is indisputable. But Freud had no training at all in anthropology and sociology; he turned to these disciplines by choice.

Beginning in 1913, *Totem and Taboo* affects a breakthrough which will be decisive in this direction. Freud returns to this area of investigation in 1921 with *Group Psychology and the Analysis of the Ego*, which immediately follows *Beyond the Pleasure Principle*. Ten years separate *Beyond the Pleasure Principle* and *Discomfort in Culture*. This time he is not driven towards this pole of thought by a swing of the pendulum. We saw that from 1920 to 1930 his reflections lead him to clarify the consequences for clinical work of the final drive theory and the structural model of the psychic apparatus and afterwards the development of the Oedipus complex, masochism, and disavowal. He goes back to the question of culture with *The Future of an Illusion* (1927), in which there is no allusion at all to the death drive. But come 1930 and we see how Freud's conviction in the truth of his theories strengthens and, far from backtracking, he annexes the field of culture. And this is what *Discomfort in Culture* represents.

We ought not be mistaken. In writing *Discomfort in Culture*, he did not think that he was engaging in anything more than an interesting digression. He could not foresee that the philosophers of May 1968 would insist that this book alone was all that remained of any value in his body of work. Several years would need to go by before we were treated a more considered reassessment of his thought. But in our time, when it is a question of the death drive, *Discomfort in Culture* cannot be overlooked. It cannot be overlooked, this much we can agree on! But can it make a claim to truth?

What, precisely, does Freud argue in *Discomfort in Culture*? First, following on from *The Future of an Illusion*, he continues his exposition of religion. That this work begins with a criticism of the ego does not surprise us. Yet again, the Darwinian Freud reveals itself pointedly. As to psychoanalysis, he pleads for the conservation of the past attested to by the survival of its traces in the ego. He inevitably examines the purpose of human existence while frustrating the illusion masking such a question, and gives it this bald reply: it concerns the aspiration to happiness and the maintenance of this state. Yet humankind is not beyond the pale of suffering. He reviews the means adopted for achieving this goal, which comes down to satisfying the drives: "The feeling of happiness derived from the satisfaction of a wild drive motion untamed by the ego is incomparably more‚intense than that derived from sating a drive that has been tamed" (Freud, 1930, p. 79).

Put differently, we experienced greater joy when we proclaimed the death of the gladiators during the Colosseum games than today when we watch the victory of a football team which we support. Sublimation has already carried out its work in one area and so pursues it elsewhere. There remains the life of the hermit. And lastly, love, that is, to love and to be loved. But this is unpredictable and risky. What of religion? It obliges psychic infantilising. Nor does the attempted harnessing of the forces of nature achieved by science suffice despite the undeniable gratifications that it procures in terms of guaranteeing our happiness. Misfortune is still all too widespread throughout humankind.

What, then, is civilisation? It designates the totality of the works and organisations whose institution distances us from the animal state and our ancestors, and which serves two ends, that is, protecting humans from nature and regulating the relations between individuals. We no longer count developments for the domination of nature. Then again, progress for resolving the problems of individual relations is more limited. One might say that culture consists, much as agriculture, in the domestication of the forces of nature in order to serve the ends of humankind. Yet the natural catastrophes which we are subject to regularly outrun us. These include earthquakes, cyclones, tsunamis, flooding, volcanic eruptions, epidemics, and so on. In reality, nature is only partially capable of being controlled.

Furthermore, not all ideologies are bearers of peace. They likewise sow death and threaten the most civilised peoples. We are endowed with law in order to limit the damage. But this may vanish from one day to the next in favour of the most obscurantist prejudices. Think of national socialism and communism. All civilisations impose on their subjects limitations on satisfying individualist drives. Freud nevertheless believes in the existence of a "civilising process" unfolding throughout humankind. Sexuality in our time seems freer than it was in Freud's. But it is never satisfied by the gains dating from recent decades. It constantly demands more freedom and even fights against the idea of "human nature", an artefact of thought, it is claimed, destined to place a limit on one's options for jouissance. Sublimation has surely gained ground, but its servants form a minority which has little purchase on the whole. Cultural renunciation imposes heavy sacrifices on the freedom of drive expression.

Freud mentions an evolutionary ideal in which Eros and Ananke[49] have become the begetters of human civilisation. But is Ananke capable of reining in Eros? Love life is a preoccupation of civilised peoples. Pornography these days nevertheless entices them, and its desire is to prevail over monogamy and family life. Freud is thus forced to ask the question concerning those tendencies opposed to erotic life which civilisation advocates. Taboos and restrictions limit the unencumbered expansion of sex life,[50] above all infantile. The greater tolerance of our age is far from encouraging its free expression

---

[49] Editor's note: In ancient Greece, Ananke was the Goddess of necessity, purpose, and inevitability.

[50] See the work of Maurice Godelier, in particular Godelier (2004).

and "constitutional" inequalities are not taken into consideration. Monogamous heterosexual love is legitimised and considered, in the vast majority of cases, to be the norm despite the very many derogations which go unnoticed or are sanctioned when they are acknowledged. Homosexuality is no longer an offence but, far from being satisfied by this outcome, homosexuals demand absolute *equality*. If nature does not give them the power to procreate, adoption corrects this limitation while waiting for biology to make it possible.

Be that as it may, the sex life of so-called civilised individuals will always be held back by the interdictions already present in non-literate societies, and in a strict enough way. In any case, sexual difference subjects our drive life to a de facto restriction. Tolerance for frustration varies in accordance with the individual. Christian morality would have us love our neighbour as we love ourselves. But are we capable of this, even if we wished to? The tendency towards taking advantage of others for our own comfort or pleasure is an unchanging observation. The preference is moreover inevitable. The fact of the other's malfeasance towards us is further hardly indisputable. Can we overcome the measure for measure which is its end result?

We observe how all of this leads Freud to the very point to which he wants to bring us, that is, to admitting the harmful effects of the death drive: "Men are not gentle creatures who want to be loved, and who at the most can defend themselves if they are attacked; they are, on the contrary, creatures among whose drive endowments is to be reckoned a powerful share of aggressiveness" (Freud, 1930, p. 111). Claiming that "the others" are like this does not suffice. We must recognise that what is so easy to condemn in others is found within ourselves. Rationality is not enough to bring us around to renouncing the aggressiveness which has been present since the dawn of humanity. The great poetic works on beginnings are war epics in which it is a matter of vanquishing and dominating an adversary who has wronged our drive satisfactions. *The Mahabharata*, *The Iliad*, and *The Ring* are among those which come to mind.

Stop for a moment and examine a single example taken from our own civilisation, *The Iliad*. Book 11 describes the third day of battle and shows the Achaeans at work. They know that they are at a disadvantage because Zeus accords his preference to the Trojans. Fully aware of this, the Achaeans work twice as hard, despite the absence of Achilles at their side. In the section which describes the exploits of Agamemnon, the "shepherd of the people", Homer delivers an inflamed narrative of the war ardour of the "lord of men" in battle. This terrible massacre of men sees the fall of a great many Trojans due to his blows as his force transforms him into a wild beast whose heightened energy, released by the combat, suggests, in light of its murderous action, a comparison with animals possessed of indomitable strength, animated as he is with impervious rage at the adversary's humanity. He brings to mind the lion which kills unrelentingly, slicing up the limbs and prying away the head of his enemies, as well as the pitiless wolf. The Atrides, "splattered with gore, his hands, invincible hands" (Homer, 1990, 11.197), pursues his prey. Not only men are opposed to Agamemnon. Zeus himself blocks his path. He is endowed with an uncommon energy, that which is appropriate for the father of the Immortals. Often, the belligerence of the combatants, caused by the death of their kin or allies, greatly increases their thirst for vengeance. This brings to mind hatred provoked and spurred on by suffering. This is not so for Agamemnon. Who can doubt here the activation of an externalised death drive whose unsurpassable example will be subsequently set by Achilles?

Seeming contrary ideologies have proven that their misdeeds were worse than those which they condemned on paper. The abolition of private property gave birth to the Gulag and the new order to the extermination camps. The country in which the Statue of Liberty is found put prisoners on a lead and torture was practiced in Algeria by the country of the French Revolution. Private property begins by appropriating objects of love. This is why it can't set limits for itself. One mustn't forget that if civilisation condemns violence, war is nonetheless monopolised by the State.

Freud at last comes to his drive theory, the final one. What he devoted himself to up to that point was what one may call clinical sociology, the second—or is it perhaps the first?—part of his drive theory which may be applied as much to the individual in clinical psychoanalysis as to all humans beings as members of the *socius*. Here we are: *Beyond the Pleasure Principle* treated biological foundations; *The Ego and the Id*, the individual in relation to his or her genitors; and *Discomfort in Culture*, the individual in society. We have come full circle.

Freud dares what few dared before him, namely, to make use of the observation of anthropological and sociological facts as if he had proceeded with clinical description; and not to encumber himself with concepts delimiting the normal and the pathological or the individual and the collective. There is but one reality alone, specifically, psychic reality observable among individuals. There can be no doubt that the tenants of these anthropological and social disciplines felt overrun, arrogated. But the aim of the Freudian enterprise is not to conquer or appropriate; rather, it aspires, without any moralising ambition, to fore-ground a previously unknown aspect of human psychic reality. Hardly any frontiers hold here; thinking is driven by highlighting what had been excluded.

The discovery of narcissism is qualified as "decisive" (Freud, 1930, p. 118), in conformity with the theory set out in *Beyond the Pleasure Principle* which introduces the death drive. This is an idea which Freud defends once again but this time around he does so unreservedly, despite the resistances (Freud's term) of his entourage: "That others should have shown, and still show, the same attitude of rejection surprises me less. For 'little children do not like it' when there is talk of the inborn human incli-nation to 'badness', to aggressiveness and destructiveness, and so to cru-elty as well" (Freud, 1930, p. 120).[51] The Devil, says Freud (ibid.), is once again the best subterfuge for exonerating God. Eros binds; the destruc-tion drives unbind. How may the desire for aggression be rendered inof-fensive? The unconscious feeling of guilt serves this goal. At this point I should like to go back to some of my own thoughts on the subject.

Freud expands on the consequences of drive renunciation (a theme he gives great importance to in *The Man Moses and Monotheistic Religion*) in *Discomfort in Culture* (Chapter 7). As it is, the renunciation of drive satisfaction is at the origin of the moral conscience (through a recapturing of the renunciation by the superego)—which, in return, always demands more. Nothing on this question is comprehensible in Freud's thinking if we leave out the idea that the erotic libido is now knotted into, and accompanied by, the aggressive and destructive libido. It befits Freud to maintain that:

---

[51] The allusion to the "little children" is drawn from a poem by Goethe.

A considerable amount of aggressiveness must be developed in the child against the authority which prevents him from having his first, but none the less his most important, satisfactions, whatever the kind of drive deprivation that is demanded of him may be; but he is obliged to renounce the satisfaction of his revengeful aggressiveness ... By means of identification he takes the un-attackable authority into himself.

(Freud, 1930, p. 129)

We now observe the difference with the "Papers on Metapsychology", which deals with the vicissitudes of the sexual drive. When the death drive props up the concept behind the manifestation of the aggressive or destructive drive, it demands something more, that is, the renunciation of drive satisfaction (in order to conserve the authority's love by bending to its interdictions). This is not a matter of repression—which would let it endure as the unconscious repressed—but a renunciation (letting-go, consent to sacrifice) of vengeful aggressiveness (potentially threatening "the life" of the object, and the loss of its love and protection). There intervene here not the inventive forms of other bindings which disguise the primitive drive demand but an *unbinding*, a letting-go in the service of the superego which will henceforth open up the way to primordial masochism. This is the death drive's *work of the negative*. It will undergo a form of partial rebinding with the superego—an agency which binds aggressiveness in the service of the sense of guilt. But Freud does not cease from insisting with regard to it that binding is incomplete; it is not consistently capable of binding anything. There remains a portion of free-floating aggressiveness which masochism seizes against the ego's interests.

(Green, 2006c; emphasis in the original)

What the appropriation of the superego agency consists in is an isolated prohibition that becomes assimilated by means of a coordinated and indisputable system, a bundle of prohibitions which reinforces its purpose for living and coherence through a secondary investment of the anonymous whole, it being unconnected to a specific individual.

Such rigour is difficult to bear and respect. This is why the psyche doesn't limit itself to it. It continues to maintain a recourse to the process of splitting, which is put to use for the circumstances. The subject serves two masters simultaneously, however contradictory they are. "My faith prohibits me from satisfying such a drive, but my desire asks of God that he accords me forgiveness for my weaknesses." A good many literary works deftly describe this split situation. In short, the pair is consistently found everywhere: the temptation to transgress the interdiction and the request for forgiveness for having done it. Should we change registers, we can see how rigid and constraining political systems apply the same recipe, that is, accusation, public confession, sanction, and repentance.

But we should note a difference. Repression defers, dissimulates, camouflages, repulses, and drives away from the conscience; renunciation abandons and lets go in order to save the object. The drive is sacrificed; the individual must extricate him- or herself from it. The reward for renunciation is obtaining the parents' love. But this comes at the price of an immense sacrifice which can but reinforce the aggressive protest against the privation of drive satisfaction.

This concept comes late in the day. Freud makes use of it in 1930 and will again use it in his testamentary work, *The Man Moses and Monotheistic Religion* (Freud, 1939). This guilty conscience tied to the superego, which Freud prefers to call the "need for self-punishment", displays its links with masochism and the negative therapeutic reaction. The notion of doing evil is not founded on the effects of drive satisfaction but on the opinion of a third party having the position of other—the parental imago whose love and protection the child expects, and which forces a renunciation of sought-after satisfaction (but at times obtained in secret).

The interiorising of authority—by virtue of the establishment of the superego—provides an explanation for this need for self-punishment. We should recall that the child's superego is moulded by the parents' superego. In other words, parents may be judged for their failures but referring to what they say that they obey, in all events, cannot be overlooked. Adversity is additionally interpreted as the punishment of a superego having godlike origins. Thus are the hardships of the Jewish people consistently accounted for by the prophets, who accuse its members of incorrect practice and/or a flawed understanding of the Torah. Fate, says Freud (1930), is thought of as a substitute for the parental agency. Consequently, anxiety faced with authority and anxiety faced with the superego come one after another. The superego observes all; nothing may be concealed from it. Whence a feeling of failing independent of the occasion in which is arises.

In the end, the need, the necessity to receive and be deserving of love, organises everything. The conscience is in fact the cause of renunciation. It is introjected.

> Here, as so often, the situation is reversed: "If I were the father and you were the child, I should treat you badly." The relationship between the superego and the ego is a return, distorted by a wish, of the real relationship between the ego, as yet undivided, and an external object. That is typical, too. But the essential difference is that the original severity of the superego does not—or does not so much—represent the severity which one has experienced from it, or which one attributes to it; it represents rather one's own aggressiveness towards it.
>
> (Freud, 1930, pp. 129–130)

We observe that the introduction of the superego in the structural model creates a kind of causality which, beside the drive component, introduces an anthropological fact, specifically, the relationship of the superego to the ego, which causes the Other to intervene. In return, the superego plunges its roots into the id. Freud will come around to defending the hypothesis of a "murder of the primitive father". So concludes his work.

The hindrance to drive satisfaction and the desire for transgression exacerbates the unconscious feeling of guilt when it is a matter of aggressive drives alone. He concludes that: "When a drive striving undergoes repression, its libidinal elements are turned into symptoms, and its aggressive components into a sense of guilt" (Freud, 1930, p. 139).

Freud is henceforth obsessed by phylogenesis, and his findings turn towards this direction. Whence the work of winding up his entire thought, *The Man Moses and Monotheistic Religion*. The process of civilising and individual development go hand in hand. They converge on the idea of putting the Father to death. Recognising this amounts, for Freud, to reaping the narcissistic satisfaction of being superior to the others, who stubbornly refuse to become conscious of it.

3.2 Primal parricide

This is a peculiar epilogue. For the years during which he worked on *The Man Moses and Monotheistic Religion*, from 1937 to 1939, the theme of the murder of the father, present in Freud's thought from 1913 (*Totem and Taboo*) and even before, broadened with a host of considerations. Clearly, it is not by chance if his life's work concludes with this book. The murder of the father is doubtless a defining theme of Freud's thinking and so the choice should come as no surprise, not even for a work which may be associated with a "historical novel" in which fiction and truth appear to blend in Freud's mind.

On the subject of this theme, Freud embroiders and inserts this core into a theoretical context which by itself may explain its importance. The reader who first studies *Discomfort in Culture* and then *The Man Moses and Monotheistic Religion* senses a seamless continuity across the theoretical discourse. A single exception stands out, however, and this concerns the absence of any mention of the death drive in the latter work.[52] *Discomfort in Culture*, though, pushes much further the role of aggressiveness triggered by the external authority which denies the subject any number of primary drive satisfactions. Still more, Freud describes the different stages which ought to mark the course of anxiety when faced with external authority, which over time evolves towards a transformation into submission when faced with the superego. Throughout this evolution, he relentlessly recalls that the source of anxiety resides in the authority that is first un-interiorised and then assimilated to the superego.

How is it that Freud, picking up on this thread of his reflection seven years later, persists in maintaining the outright importance of the role of the religious superego without saying a word about how the destruction drives come into play? Here we return to an Oedipus in which are

---

[52] Whereas elsewhere, notably in *Discomfort in Culture*, he speaks of the murder of the united brothers in terms of sadism.

present the manifestations of rivalry and opposition between child and parents but in which the dynamic source, that is to say, the action of the destructive drives, is not explicitly mentioned. Notwithstanding, recently discovered facts, such as drive renunciation, are the subject of a more advanced theorisation. "Progress in the life of the mind" is associated with the difference between evidence by the senses, associated with the mother, and the evidence due to the progress of spirituality[53]— deductions, inferences, and implications—associated with the father. There can be no doubt that this is something of an enigma, which cannot be readily resolved. Here we need to delve into this puzzle to try and understand the idea underlying the theory.

For Freud, the basic conflict—that between the child (most often he only discusses the boy) and the interdicting authority, the castrating father—needs to be defined. It is reasonable to assert that, in his view, the conflict between the child, dominated by drives seeking nothing other than their satisfaction, and the obstacle to drive gratification constitutes a fundamental complex. There stems from this the threat of castration and the formation of the superego, which is the generator of unconscious guilt and the need for punishment. What remains in a state of investigation is the conflict's source. Is it caused by the aggressive potency belonging to the destruction drives or does it suffice to appreciate the intensity of the conflict by its phylogenetic reference or the ineluctability of its appearance?

Freud scarcely asks the question and even less so suggests an answer. Rather, his deep, unshakable conviction about the phylogenetic component of his thesis is affirmed twice rather than once. Which explains the religious response. Following the enslavement in Egypt, it is no longer pharaoh who is feared but rather the volcano god, Yahweh. We recall that monotheism, justifying the omnipotence of God, originates in the ephemeral religion of Akhenaten, who ruled for but a short time since the priests had reassumed power on his death and re-established the old religion which had empowered them. Following the pharaoh's death they eradicated, suppressed, and radically censured anything

---

[53] Translator's note: In French, *spiritualité*. Freud's German is *Geistigkeit* which, in Y. H. Yerushalmi's gloss, "hovers between *intellectuality* and *spirituality*" (Yerushalmi, 1991, p. 51; emphasis in the original).

that made any mention of him by hammering away any monument that referred to him.

In short, the same conflict was continuously played out between a new form of ethical power ousting that which preceded it, followed by its own fall from power aiming at re-establishing the old symbols of its sovereignty. In other words, a new power seeks to overthrow a former power to its advantage and takes vengeance on it by persecuting the young adepts, which is then followed by the return of the former power.

This conflictual tangle doubtless becomes, for Freud, at least in this book, more important than the drive nature of the forces bidding to seize power. This is what may be deduced from the strange omission in *The Man Moses and Monotheistic Religion*. The New Testament extends the Old, certainly, but it also ensures its hegemony over it. Jesus dethrones Moses and Christians would long persecute Jews. Even later, Islam, the youngest of the three monotheisms, will lay claim *a posteriori* to its superiority. And so there we are. Perhaps, however, the ancestral parricide succeeded in effacing any trace of its presence.

Death acknowledges a disavowal since in this case no drive conveys it. Its violence nevertheless remains redoubtable, destructive, irrational, fanatic. Hope for a compromise which makes these three monotheisms compatible, allowing them to coexist in peace, seems but an illusion.

The conclusion of *The Man Moses and Monotheistic Religion*, which is, further, the final word in Freud's work, has wide reach. Against any naive geneticism which tends to grant greater importance to what is older, Freud adopts a structural view: *Prima* passes behind *Summa*. And *Summa* is nothing other than the figure of the Father. This is one of the formidable issues of psychoanalysis in our time, which seems to repeat the Court of the Areopagus that judged Orestes. Freud is, however, the father and this is what he proclaims loud and clear. There is no need then to adhere, as now, to the observations of children who, with a single voice, seek to demonstrate the primacy of the mother. Freud well knows that she exists, but it appears that he wishes to say that the father is something else, he who represents the "progress of the life of the mind" and who animates cultural life, and this is the reference humankind requires in order, at the right time, to rise up against him, revolt, put him to death, and express remorse over it. Nothing similar exists with regard to the mother. It is not that matricide is overlooked, and incest even less so. But actual incest is rarely the occasion for cultural achievements and putting the mother to death knows no penalty other than madness.

So then, it comes down to choosing castration anxiety and fear of the father rather than fragmentation and seduction by the mother. And then there is also the veneration of the father, the respect he deserves, the homages paid to him. The father is the dead father. The dead mother is something else, namely, an infinite, constantly recurrent depression opposed to life.

3.3 Recent discussions on cultural process

The ideas expressed by Freud in *Discomfort in Culture* have been the subject of recent exchanges. A debate at the UNESCO colloquium organised by the Paris Psychoanalytic Society several years ago, moderated by Jean-Louis Baldacci, pitted Nathalie Zaltzman against Jean-Luc Donnet (Donnet & Zaltzman, 2003). Zaltzman underscored the parallelism between the civilising progress and progress due to the cure while Donnet resolutely aligned himself with Freudian pessimism.

The pre-Freudian conception of humankind traditionally sees in it the effect of a difference in nature with animals by virtue of the presence of spiritual transcendence. Whether this is an acquisition of the evolution of the preceding species and expressed in the essential depths of humanity or the result of a strict subduing of the drives, the outcome is the same: humankind is endowed with spiritual force. Freud's theses combat this idea. First because it follows along a continuous line of descent with animals. And then, when we compare humans with animals, the former appear considerably more invested by drive elements because the difference between the instinct and the drives enriches them with all the resources of ruse and intelligence maintained in the service of their goals.

Another blunt observation is that culture, far from succeeding in "humanising" humans, most often fails. Civilisation does not get the better of barbarism. The latter may see its forces revive and attain unsuspected heights in times when this seems inconceivable. We need only think of the Shoah. This is what one calls Freudian pessimism, about which Freud replied, when queried, that it was so only in relation to the exaggerated optimism of his adversaries. In short, he carried on to the end the disillusioning enterprise which, for him, constitutes the aim of psychoanalysis.

Jean-Luc Donnet (1995, 1998), who worked on the question of the superego and the relationship of the cultural process to sublimation, considers them in terms of the work of culture. Whereas for the individual the principal aim remains the attainment and preservation of the advantages accorded to the drives, for the cultural process the establishment of a unity stretching across individuals is the priority. The conclusion is obvious: specifically, the maintaining of cohesion within the group by means, among others, of mutual identifications unifying individuals.

The disparity between the individual superego and the cultural superego is thus due to the different goals they pursue. One nevertheless refers to the other as the first reflects the long-term temporality of the species while the second, which depends on generational transmission, ensures continuity between generations. The child's superego is built upon the parents'. The images appreciated by each culture make the group and individual dimensions communicate with each other. In this instance, intergenerational transmission comes into play.

This particular cultural aim distances us still further from our early, animal condition. Humans must thus accept an increasingly greater dose of frustration—a theme which we have gone into at length. How are we to compensate these losses of satisfaction? It seems that renunciation never finds compensation equal to the sacrifices to which it must consent. We will not go into those required by the satisfaction of the sexual drives. As an ever-present impulse in humans, the drive requires continuous attention. Within Eros, the constituent drive categories replace one another. Sublimation, the vicissitudes of the drives, extends the pathway of the displacements of goals, which are associated with the privileged investment of the higher psychic activities (ethics, religion, and so on), extends the pathway of the displacements of goals. I should emphasise that we as humans are not only dependent on our primal animality, but this further takes on in us a shade of madness. On this point I refer to my discussion in "Between madness and psychosis" (in Green, 1990).

The sexualisation of all the psychic processes finds in this the opportunity for vengeance. We have seen that the discovery of the destructive drives but widens the field of renunciation, the principal source of unconscious guilt. The defensive ensembles, denial–splitting–projection, and the idealisation–persecution pair (Melanie Klein), assist in the transformation of the primal drive forms. In the end, these outcomes must be assessed with regard to illusion: "The superego, because it is an agency that is as irreducible to the ego as is the id, constitutes a repository of illusions" (Donnet, in Donnet & Zaltzman, 2003, p. 228).

Analytic work may be compared to the work of culture. The over-investment of the higher psychic functions (the reference to "truth") is constantly observed. Reflections on the place of the healing process among analytic values follows. For Donnet, this remains "on top of it", an addition.

This individual–collective interface is problematic. The cultural superego and its ideals blend their effects by respecting their mutual spaces. Nathalie Zaltzman, in dialogue with Jean-Luc Donnet, sees in the two works, that of the cure and that of culture, a surfeit of psychic expenditure since the essential feature, pleasure, cannot be replaced. Thus, the effort to be made in order to invest the unpleasure of sacrifice is inevitably greater. Eros and Ananke are called upon to contribute. Zaltzman (ibid., p. 212) emphasises that the direct character of the satisfactions is of lesser importance than that of another priority: "It [human evolution] affects its investment of its experiences of pleasure and suffering only through what they represent in the economy of desire of the other."

I may take the opportunity at this point to recall one of my thoughts on "psychic causality", specifically, that it does not fall uniquely under the natural sciences nor under the anthropological human sciences. I would also like to recall in passing the reference to Lacan's "Big Other", an Outside the Self agency. We should relate this to the cultural superego (Diatkine, 2000). At just the right moment the Outside the Self echoes Freud's conceptions on the civilising process as "overarching humanity". This process must base itself on the values of the investment, of the recognition, associated with the defences, repression, foreclusion, denial, destruction, and self-destruction. Freud himself brings the cultural process of humanity and the process of individual development or education together. It comes down to an effect of Eros, then. Zaltzman cannot bring herself to adopt the viewpoint of Freudian pessimism, despite the Eros–Thanatos opposition. It seems to me that by appealing to the surfeit of investment, she returns to Freud's final ideas, those which acknowledge the link between the encompassing work of the life drives in search of increasingly vast syntheses and the inescapable swelling of tensions that this implies.

In conclusion, if Jean-Luc Donnet is correct in recalling with Walter Benjamin "the immemorial failure of culture in the domain of human relations", Nathalie Zaltzman, in reference to my own work, emphasises that in our day there exists appreciably more truth than ever before among individuals. But it is further true that truth is not always victorious over lies and the destructive action that this very action seeks to foster.

To put things briefly, then. On the one hand, we find a fidelity to Freudian pessimism while on the other, an open-mindedness to hope just as quickly recused.

What, then, should we make of this?

3.4 The death drive and language: Laurence Kahn

In our outline of the arguments that have preceded, we distinguished the voices of those who did not consider the death drive as true from those who, with and like Freud, did accept it, and further those who while taking into account the drive dialectic felt the need inspired by Lacan to associate it with an Outside the Self, a Nobody (as per Homer) or the Big Other—whose links with Speech or the Name-of-the-Father were explicitly mentioned or could be implicitly sensed.

We may now examine an important development which we owe to Laurence Kahn. Her recent book, *Speak, Destiny*, gives it a name. As an analyst well-versed in the parsing of texts and concepts, Kahn (2005) rightly intends to shift the debate, and so she succeeds. Till now we have shown the positions of those who share Freud's pessimism. Likewise, Kahn cannot be accused of defending the cause of illusion. While psychoanalysis has been associated with the endeavour to free the psyche from the chains of repression, lo and behold she changes tack and asks us to abandon all hope owing to the power of the destruction drives. Is analysis worthless when faced with the power of death? Psychoanalysts have indeed thought that Freud wanted to lead them in this direction, and yet they opposed it and resisted the temptation of despair.

The spirit of the times near the end of his life, which alas saw the coming of Nazism, scarcely encouraged illusion. The final part of

The Man Moses and Monotheistic Religion, in which Freud discovers the unnatural alliance between progress and barbarism, attests to this. It is true that *Discomfort in Culture* is not an isolated work. Valéry warned us that civilisations were mortal, but he did not go so far as to proclaim that they could commit suicide. Other thinkers, among them Husserl and Spengler, alerted us to the crisis in European civilisation. But none singled out the death drive. Be that as it may, the faith that the eighteenth-century Enlightenment gave birth to was highly excessive. Foreseeing that the political regimes of 1914–1918 would witness the collapse of humanist reason was problematic.

Yet, we have explained, Freud did not act precipitously in 1920. He waited until 1930 in order to show what had become certain—and so he would until he died. If we wish to trace the origins of the 1920 watershed, we must arguably emphasise the recusal of the concept of the unconscious and its replacement by that of the id shortly afterwards. In other words, it was a matter of affirming the observations on the shortcomings of a system founded on *unconscious representations* and replacing them with an id constrained to adopt a more economic and energetic conception at the basis of which is accentuated the role of *drive motions* (Green, 2006b). This represents yet another retreat in relation to feeble reason, which once again finds itself outdone. Freud nevertheless does not cease from putting his gifts in its service, provided that it consents to renouncing its illusions. As Kahn says,

> Making *destiny* speak is thinking's line of resistance when it brings into opposition, on the one hand, belief and violence and, on the other, the search for causes; when it enters into the description of all forms of human distress and their treatment by the individual and community.
>
> (Kahn, 2005, p. 16)

It seems that Freud's Darwinism, which is consistently present yet unobtrusive, takes precedence without yielding anything to the "human" legacy bequeathed by our fathers. At the meeting-point of both is a form of psychoanalytic experience which has fallen away from Romantic mysticism of any kind. According to Kahn, Freud remains close to Kant, a point further explicitly postulated by Bion but in a quite different way.

How can we put our trust in thinking when, analysed and no longer analyst, it displays such scarcely rational unconscious determinations?

The "soul's apparatus" is a provocative choice of words. The soul consisting of an apparatus is a contradiction in terms. Such was the project of Freud's physicalist friends on the cusp of his lifework. To a certain extent this appears in the course of his initial formulations on hysteria. But this dispute should not lead us astray. The language of the "Project for a scientific psychology" does not run counter to that of Freud's initial psychic breakthroughs. The "Project for a scientific psychology" does not exclude hysteria, which on the contrary forms an integral part of it. That hysteria cannot be reduced to what this essay says about it is true. It goes well beyond it, as what happens next in Freud's work shows. The relative autonomy of the psyche attests to this. If the soul is "higher" than the nervous system, it is no less anchored *in* it. Not as a cerebral localisation but as the other side of the frontier in which the drive sits, at the intersection of body and soul. This is a point where philosophy stalls. Does the soul, a borderline concept, sit at an intersection? The soul falls within the realm of the drives: it is the sublimation of the movement operating in the psyche, and this is a concept that goes against the tide of accepted truths.

Time and again have we listened to the chorus of philosophers lamenting Freud's regrettable biological leanings. What a pity, such an intelligent man! And, at the other end, a like chorus consisting of the tenants of biology making up the adverse clan. What a pity, such an intelligent man! If only he'd pursued the bright ideas in the "Project for a scientific psychology"! We see how Freud throws them back-to-back. Neither opens their reasoning up to what he calls *drive motions*. In contradistinction to his critics, he well observed their effects on himself while at the same time observing them in others, first and foremost his patients. We should not let ourselves be charmed by the habits of mind which blur our vision. I have known Nobel laureates who continued to proclaim publicly that "It's all charlatanism! I maintain and repeat that I don't have an unconscious!"[54] Freud fought his whole life long for a provision of convincing proof. And what may be said about

---

[54] See the delectable exchange with Jacques Monod related by Gerald Edelman (1992).

post-hypnotic suggestion? Are we still going to believe the individual who out of the blue opens an umbrella in front of us after a session of hypnosis in which he was instructed to do so and who, when asked about why he'd done it, replies, "To see if it worked"?

But it is true that along the way we also meet up with some genuine questions. We are encouraged to return to the "demonic" in taking account of its effects one after another. In other words, there is nothing Romantic in this *analytic* project which requires an extension of the traditional limits of reason and its forms of expression, particularly those in which we perceive the mark of the sexual. In short, it amounts to settling the Devil back beside the "Good" Lord.

Laurence Kahn refuses to make Freud cross over to the side of energetics—whose role, however, is constantly emphasised by him, in particular after 1923—as she is consistently suspicious of trying to naturalise his thinking. She writes: "The primal drive is the primary foundation of representation, which implies that the drive, this drive of reason, is not engendered by objects but that it engenders its own object" (Kahn, 2005, p. 52).[55] Thus is justified the distinction that Kahn puts forward between presentation and representation, that is, the effect of a drive of reason. This remark is less philosophical and more "Freudian" than it seems since presentation is a presentation of the senses whereas representation is a representation of the drive. Whence the reference to

---

[55] Editor's note: After the publication of the French version of this book, in an exchange of letters, Laurence Kahn objected to the way in which Green had phrased this sentence. She felt that it could be misinterpreted by readers to imply that it was not Schlegel's position she was describing but her own. Green apologised and defended himself by saying he did not mean to imply that Kahn "agreed" with Schlegel and the German Romantics or "asserted" a similar view, but only that Kahn had "written", meaning *written about*, the Schlegel position, which she factually had done. As their correspondence continued, however, there seemed to be a more important difference at issue in regard to borderline or limit cases.

According to Kahn (personal communication, 2022), Green (1999) believed in the existence of feeling states dominated by confused, uncontrollable affective movements, apparently unbound by any representation. He therefore hypothesized "raw forms"—perceived by the analyst—that refer to "the expression of a raw drive force". Kahn insists that the affect is always a "delegate" or representative of the drive and so does not agree that the form can be the direct refraction of the force as Green proposed.

aesthetics and the note on *Witz*—"wit", "spirit-born wit". Recall that in this work Freud distinguishes between the spirit of the tendency (the future drive, in my view) and the spirit of words (words of the drive, again in my view). One may thus say that the death drive is the spirit of death. Kahn is committed to bringing out how much Freud's approach affects a break with Romanticism. This is hardly astonishing as Freud never missed the opportunity to recall his own adherence to a scientific viewpoint. Is it the only one which disillusions? Yes, on condition that science does not yield to the power of illusion which disillusion gives birth to in return.

"How may language gain access to the language of what lies beyond language?" As a reply, do we only have reasons? According to Wittgenstein, "What we cannot speak about, we must pass over in silence" (Wittgenstein, 1971, p. 151). Adopting this comes quite easily, to which Charcot had already replied, "This doesn't prevent one from existing."[56]

Take an example and listen to psychotic speech. Then compare the differing non-psychotic speech running counter to it in order to grasp its meaning. Unless we ordain that such speech is bereft of meaning, non-psychotic speech does not prove capable of offering an acceptable translation of what the psychotic says. Neither the psychiatrist nor the phenomenologist nor the cognitive-behaviourist can make sense of the language that such a patient speaks and whose grammar we are igno-rant of. Are we to be counted among the "organicists"? Forced to make brain structures speak, we understand still less what is in question.

We should admit that the drive is destiny. But then, which destiny is reserved for the death drive? And for a start, we ought to realise that denial of the death drive—first of all, by Freud—lasted longer than denial of the sexuality of Eros about which we ended up by thinking that it by itself held the keys to drive life. The illusion seeped into theory and this but postponed disillusionment, even if it did not impede it. Barbarism, that is, war, returned and made it necessary to think the unthinkable. *Discomfort in Culture* would force us to do so. The ten-dency to dislocation prevails over its obstacles. Look at the question of violence. Freud sets Einstein straight on this point since it is a matter

---

[56] Translator's note: This is an allusion to Freud's comments on Charcot's remark men-tioned in Freud (1893, p. 13).

of violence not power (*Macht*), as the physicist suggests in drawing an opposition between *Recht* (law) and *Macht*. The Enlightenment was but one more utopia and Freud himself subscribed to it. Does Laurence Kahn sufficiently locate the internal mutation which in 1923 accompanied the *recusal* of the unconscious by Freud and the option supporting drive *motions* against unconscious *representations*, whence stems the triumph of the concept of force without which Freudian thought is mutilated?

The death drive, that is, the ultimate expression of self-hatred. The death drive, after all is said and done, is suicidal. What we must concede is the *pair* consisting of construction–destruction, of love–hate, in antagonism and agonism on the grounds that we are shaped by this pair. All we are considering is nothing other than their intrication and disintrication.

Kahn argues the hypothesis—which she recognises as such—that "the new culture of borderline cases, the new odyssey of analytic courage, is as one with the heroism that any epic narrative fosters" (Kahn, 2005, p. 230). But does psychoanalysis, herald of Eros, have any other choice from the moment destructiveness sets up camp on the field? For Kahn, it would be a matter of misrecognition. Unless thinking that the concealment which underpins her own position is the true misrecognition of a nostalgic psychoanalysis. Kahn in fact comes to the rescue of imperilled language, but is it not the psychoanalysts who have put it into danger by desiring to ignore "language's other"? Ignoring the impact of borderline cases is equivalent to making madness and psychosis "illnesses" of language, which, I fear, they are not and have never been. Borderline cases and borderline disorders of the personality are clinical figures rising out of contemporary pathology—which the analyst must take into account in his or her practice, and not feign to ignore them— and not inventions rising out of the imagination of certain analysts. Ah, how sunny neurosis was compared to the weather under the borderline cases! What are we thinking of? Of the patients in the *Studies on Hysteria*? Of the Wolf Man?

At this point we reach a dividing line. It is perhaps not irrelevant whether or not the reader of this work was a psychiatrist, a practitioner who frequented the undeniable horror of mental illness and its socalled asylums. For a psychiatrist, the memory remains, but someone who has no acquaintance of it would, on the contrary, have no recollection of it. Such an individual has never seen a mentally ill person confined for a full year to a cell—this is how their room was called—in which all furniture was removed since as a matter of course it would be smashed to pieces and whose bed was no more than an indestructible metal frame, pacing around like a lion in a cage, be it windy or snowing, howling for days on end, getting their food through a mere hatch and who no hospital attendant would be permitted to approach or speak to since they would be attacked even before they had the time to open their mouth. Such an experience is quite familiar to me. Whoever doesn't know what it means to be mad, in the sense of a destructive psychosis, should think twice before speaking and passing the slightest judgement. The reader might ask, "Come now, what does all that have to do with my patients in analysis?" Nothing and everything. But that does not prevent us from analysing tragedies. Are we talking about psychiatric terrorism or cultural terrorism? I myself see it as the terrorism of destructiveness in action.

The return to biology: apoptosis or self-programmed natural death

Let's state it straight away. Adding a section on biology to a book devoted to the death drive might give rise to a mistaken interpretation, if one hopes to surmise that the author's aim is to gain purchase on science in order to shore up a hypothesis which is far from originating in it directly. Notwithstanding, we should recall that the death drive's opponents have long propped themselves up on science in order to insist on the viewpoint of its impossibility. We are not at present maintaining that science comes to the rescue of those who champion this hypothesis. On the other hand, we can see in the theses of modern biology something novel which, at the very least, says nothing which expressly contradicts it. Jean Claude Ameisen published a book in 1999, *The Sculpture of Living Things: Cell Suicide and Creative Death*, which opened up new avenues in biological thinking. We have read correctly, cell *suicide*, which obliges us to consider the suicide which the cell itself commits, that is to say, how it may be observed as an order to self-destruct.

Early work reaches back to 1885 (Walther Flemming's "chromatolysis"). It was later followed in 1951 by Alfred Glücksmann's "cell death". Their real significance was not recognised at the time. It was not until the end of the 1960s that the concepts of "programmed death" and "cell suicide" appeared. It was then discovered how cell death was programmed down to the most precise modalities of its realisation:

> It is because cell death is suicide—an active phenomenon of self-destruction—and not the result of brutal murder or paralysis that it may be complemented by a discourse on precise emission of signals and messages; and it does not take place in complete silence or an indistinct hubbub or clamour.
>
> (Ameisen, 1999, p. 65)

Ameisen doesn't shy away from metaphor and speaks of complex funeral rites at the very instant of programmed cell death: "The living world eliminates the dead. The living world eats the dead" (Ameisen, 1999, p. 66). And further, apoptosis is a process "of the methodical self-effacement" (Ameisen, 1999, p. 67).

The processes of self-destruction thus heed signals, quite like the process of creation. Regarding this point, the trophoblasts form a bridge between the mother and child prior to becoming radically differentiated. One after another, the division which engenders the multitude, the differentiation whence is born diversity and migration (the movement of cells throughout the body), punctuates each stage. In parallel are produced "natural" disappearances, a disconcerting discovery having to do with a mysterious cause. What's the purpose of these deaths? Here's the answer: "The deconstruction of the body, as it builds itself, is one of the essential components of the development of complexity" (Ameisen, 1999, p. 30). At each developmental stage, death *sculpts* the form of the embryo. This process makes possible the creation of an internal space. The brain and immune system are the most complex structures in our organism. They share a property which guarantees the longevity of our singular identity—and the construction of a history.[57] And if we were not apprehensive about the sniggers of some of our readers, we would say, "Oh yes, narcissism and the final drive theory".

The importance of the connections between the cell and its entourage is astonishing. As Ameisen writes:

---

[57] This explains why we are not surprised that an immunologist (Edelman, 1992) has suggested the most compelling ideas on brain functioning.

A receptor [of the immune system] entirely incapable of interacting with the self cannot transmit any signal to the lymphocyte which bears it for three days. And the absence of any signal, and it alone, will trigger the death of the lymphocyte which shows its incapacity to interact with sentinel cells—the proof of its likely future uselessness.

(Ameisen, 1999, p. 47)

Moving on to the brain, we find a surprising parallel. In the regions and nerves in the process of being established, half of the neurons setting out in search of partners will die during the period in which the synapses are formed. The death rate may be as high as 85 per cent but sometimes only 10 to 20 per cent. All neurons have been programmed to die. What is at stake is the setting-up of a narrow contact with a partner. The "relation" triumphs over the individual isolate. Those which have established aberrant connections are likewise subject to the fatal outcome. There exist not only forms of the sculpted body but also sculpted brains.

Ameisen writes:

The grandmasters of chess devise their moves according to grand schemas and the predominant positions on the chessboard: the openings, which are limited in number, are inventoried in their minds with precision, as are the endgames. But the game's progress is an open question and renewed each time.

(Ameisen, 1999, p. 55)

Is Ameisen aware that Freud made the same observation concerning the analytic cure?[58] The defining role of the game proceeds through the creation of conditions of evolving self-organisation. "A cell's destiny depends on the quality of its temporary ties that it weaves with its environment" (Ameisen, 1999, p. 55).

---

[58] Translator's note: "Anyone who hopes to learn the noble game of chess from books will soon discover that only the openings and endgames admit an exhaustive systematic presentation and that the infinite variety of moves which develop after the opening defy any such description" (Freud, 1913, p. 123).

In brief, we might believe that attempting to define the processes which characterise life consist in appreciating a continuous creation, without destruction. Complexity obliges us however to rethink this schema and understand that complexity includes both construction and destruction.

Is Freud and his final drive theory so far removed from this process? I do not believe so.

> At any moment each of our cells possesses throughout the length of its existence the power to destroy itself in merely several hours. And the survival of the ensemble of the cells making us up—our own survival—depends on their capacity to find in the environment of our body the signals which permit them to suppress, day after day, the activation of their suicide.
>
> (Ameisen, 1999, p. 13)

Our sentence is thus suspended; life is but the neutralising of self-destructive powers: "a positive event—life—is born out of the negation of a negative event—self-destruction" (Ameisen, 1999, p. 13).

In brief, it's a matter of coming to grips with looking death in the eye with a view to renouncing any intentionality. "The evolution of living things also exposes the price of its brilliant efficiency: a blind and absolute indifference to becoming, to freedom, and to the suffering of each of its components" (Ameisen, 1999, p. 17).

The description of the stages of programmed cell death is impressive. Approximately fifteen proteins make it possible to cut into pieces those which are indispensable for the cell's survival. This action provokes the condensation and fragmentation of the cell in the process of dying under the influence of genetic variations. The cell is divided between an executioner and a protector.

Spores present a form of intermediary life. They are representations of a form of life slowed-down, between life and death, and potentially capable of becoming fully living once more.

Blocking cell death isn't always an advantage, as the prospect of cancers shows. It is thus appropriate to activate this self-destructive process by unblocking it. The term apoptosis was proposed in 1972 by John Kerr, an anatomical pathologist, and Andrew Wyllie. Based on the comparison with "necrosis", apoptosis nevertheless presents singular characteristics:

> Whereas necrosis gives the impression of an explosive phenom-
> enon, apoptosis resembles an implosive phenomenon. The cell
> which activates its suicide first begins by cutting off all contact
> with its environment. Like an animal in the process of dying,
> the cell detaches and isolates itself from neighbouring cells. It
> then breaks up in a methodical manner: it condenses and then
> fragments its nucleus, cutting up the ensemble of its genes'
> library into small bits. At the same time, the cell body also con-
> denses itself and then disassembles itself into tiny balloons, the
> "apoptotic bodies". The cell's external membrane is modified
> and takes on the appearance of blebbing while remaining intact
> and impeding the liberating towards the outside of the enzymes
> that it contains, and avoiding any surrounding destruction.
> This quick, solitary, and calm death typically doesn't lead to any
> lesion, inflammation, or cicatrisation. The surrounding cells fill
> in the space left free by the dead ones. By and by no trace of the
> quick, controlled work of self-destruction will remain.
>
> (Ameisen, 1999, pp. 62–63)

"Draw the curtain, the farce is over."[59]

We must accustom ourselves to the banality of death. A statistic presses itself upon us: more than 99 per cent of the species in existence for the past four billion years have in all likelihood become extinct for all time. This does not impede death from remaining a source of anxiety for the human race in general and for all living humans in particular.

---

[59] Translator's note: François Rabelais's last words are said to be, "Je m'en vais chercher un Grand Peut-être. Tirez le rideau, la farce est jouée." (I'm going to seek a Great Perhaps. Draw the curtain, the farce is over.)

Leave-taking, updated

More than eighty-five years have now gone by since the concept of the death drive was advanced and more than sixty-five years since Freud was alive to defend it against his critics. We've seen how his belief in it strengthened from 1920 up until his death in 1939. And yet his own eyes never witnessed the destruction of the Jews of Europe in the Nazi concentration camps, the Soviet "re-education" camps, the damage caused by the atomic bomb in Asia, or the fate of the opponents of Pol Pot's regime in Cambodia.

These are sorrowful confirmations of an idea born out of his intuitions. Nothing about it made it possible to hope that the danger could be averted; on the contrary, the facts have only confirmed Freud's worst apprehensions. And yet we're only keeping to the principal facts.

When considering clinical practice, whatever theory one holds or has elaborated, in contemporary psychoanalysis it is always a matter of coming to terms with destructiveness, the new arrival among the clinical forms treated by psychoanalysts. Freud himself pointed out three illustrative instances of the death drive: the unconsciousness of guilt, masochism, and the negative therapeutic reaction. While these observations are hardly debatable, modern clinical practice adds quite a few others to them.

Updating the concept of the death drive is far from easy. First, due to the mass of data which one must fit in; since it isn't only a matter of challenging Freud's interpretations so as to envisage other less speculative solutions but further everything that belongs to post-Freudian literature, whose diverse positions may be poorly reducible to any unifying idea. Furthermore, we must consider all that contemporary clinical practice has taught us and which Freud missed, with everything this gives rise to in terms of variations on technique or making provision for new parameters.

Chief among them is a question that is at once terminological and conceptual. Pointing to sexuality as a manifestation of the sex drives has, it seems, never shocked anyone, nor has their replacement by Eros raised any objections. But speaking about the death *drive* arouses reactions of quite a different kind.

Perhaps we must be clear and explain that death and the death drive are different things. Death is a fact. It is scientifically attested. It is defined by objective signs (a flat electroencephalogram for a certain duration, and so on) which anyone may observe. And we quite well know that when we prolong—sometimes for several years—the existence of a person who is truly living dead, this is a matter of artifice. A simple disconnecting dissipates the illusion of artificial life still lingering on. But a drive which pushes towards death can by no means be taken for granted. What do we mean by this? If we avoid the controversial term of death drive and above all recall that if it is a question of (self- and hetero-) destruction, then things become clearer.

The destruction of what? The destruction of life, certainly, that is, the destruction of the physical, animate body which lives and breathes—since, concerning life and the soul, we immediately identify death by the cessation of respiration (*pneuma*). But, further, the destruction of the soul and psyche, which is in itself more difficult to appreciate since we anyhow suspect life of being masked by appearances. The destruction of the soul is what any initiative of servitude and domination in war which pits itself against the other—the foreign(er), the bad, and the hated—seeks. There can be no triumph over the other if the other is left to think freely and, given half a chance, to hold the enemy in contempt. What is sought is the surrender of anything which seems to fall under individual will and which is entitled to express difference, the rejection of or opposition to the other.

Perhaps we must distinguish, as I've tried to do, between paternal masochism (suffering *for* the father) and maternal masochism, in which the mother sacrifices everything in order to spare the child from suffering (the mother's sense of sacrifice). In fact, the two merge: it is a matter of reaching the point of the forgetting of self-preservation in order to serve an image placed above all else (God, the child). Questioning the validity of the designation of the drive is less justified than recalling that everything starts from the repetition compulsion, beyond the pleasure principle. In this instance, the drive thus means a primitive organisation on which the ego has no hold and which tends to reproduce itself without actually being related to the repetitive quest for pleasure but aims, according to Freud, at re-establishing a prior state.

The (death) drive exists because Freud needed one in order to integrate it into his theoretical system. The real question then becomes: Is the drive a subject for serious reflection? From the moment that the contents of his concept reinforce the coherence of his theory, what remains is secondary. What is important is the construction–destruction pair, along with its intrication–disintrication correlate. There are in fact two ways of conceiving the death drive. The fact of cases attesting to an uncontrollable aspiration to failure, unpleasure, or suffering; this is a limited application which finds its justification without too much difficulty. Next there are the goals of the Eros–destruction drive pair, an application which is broader and suggests a novel vision of psychic life.

When I find myself, in analysis, faced with particular forms of the unconscious feeling of guilt, masochism, and extreme negative therapeutic reaction, I try to account for them. But when, going beyond the frame, I think about the meaning of the unconscious feeling of guilt, masochism, or other forms of negativity encountered in the cure, I tell myself that *ultimately* everything is connected to manifestations of the death drive. And if I've come to this conclusion, it isn't in relation to some reality which I might capture in my net but because I recognise the essentially speculative nature of this "paramount" concept, as Freud called it. And he asserted the right that paramount concepts need not be proved. Is this then a question of an imaginary "biologism" or metabiology that dares not speak its name? It's rather the search for a conceptual coherence constituent of the psyche.

A point in question arises, however. I'm unable to decide if the essential nature of the death drive has an internal origin, aiming at the subject's death, or if its external orientation aiming at the other's death is primary. It seems to me that experience is too poor a guide for reaching a conclusion. What seems important to me is the paradigm of primal destructiveness possessing a dual orientation and which most often remains unconscious. I have pointed out elsewhere (Green, 2000, p. 166) that when raising a very young child, one must be mindful that, through mistreatment, the death drive does not devastate the experience of living.

Extending this thesis, I would say that when painful experiences frustrate the pleasure principle and overwhelm the psyche, they result in experiences of unrepresentable destructiveness owing to their all-out, devastating power, that is, external and internal. Deadly anxiety and limitless destruction fill the entire psyche. *The daimonic becomes demonic*. Our understanding is that in such cases we cannot speak of regression to a prior libidinal state but that it is a matter of comprehensive regression in which destructiveness is unable to face psychic pain, nor put a stop to it.

In brief, we're closer to what Pierre Marty calls disorganisation than regression, strictly speaking. Pleasure is likewise irrelevant here; paradoxically, only jouissance reigns. It is uninterpretable; in other words, interpretations remain ineffective over it. Whatever the case, I feel obliged to make reference to the idea of a drive force in the sense of a cyclone that nothing may stop. This is doubtless brought about by the feeling of an ego reduced to impotence, just like the analyst when he or she becomes the object of such tempestuous reactions, without the feeling of having provoked them. We should not forget the role, in less extreme forms, of libidinal co-excitation.

There remain a few points to be discussed stemming from the aforementioned. This is the inadequacy of the taking into consideration of the object's role in this situation's creation, and which has become accepted fact. Winnicott tried to remedy this. We should not forget the essential role of intrication (the object's principal contribution) and potential disintrication in which is marked its failure.

To conclude, we shall draw out several aspects:

1) Contrary to what Freud leads us to believe, the death drive implies neither supremacy in relation to the life drive nor definitive irreversibility when it happens to gain the upper hand.
2) In a normal state, intrication stimulated by the object is the form by which it must be sensed. However, I believe that one may observe it in an all-but-entirely disintricated state (anorexia).
3) The death drive must take into account its complementary pole, that is, the object relation on which to a great extent it depends.
4) The experience of transference may succeed in rebinding what was unbound while swayed by the death drive. The analyst's role in the transference cannot be minimised. It depends on its primal model, the object.
5) The field of the death drive is inner or outer. It reaches across criminological psychopathy and the psychosomatoses.

Whatever the options adopted by one or the other—since no decisive argument may settle the question—,the fact remains—and this is what is essential to admit—that today we must acknowledge the *centrality of the concept of destruction*. To be sure, this may be interpreted in different ways, but the crux of the matter is that it must not be masked.

The reflection on the sociocultural field and psycho-criminality is developed in order to remind us of this. I've tried to describe an objectualising function whose goal is to transform functions into objects, another way of describing the work of Eros, and, by means of correlation, a disobjectualising function whose role consists in making objects indifferent to their use in terms of jouissance and destructiveness. Drive and object likewise form an indissociable pair.

Tentative conclusion

This book does not contain any case reports. It is nonetheless nourished by my psychoanalytic experience. I've desisted from this because the work would have doubled in size if I'd used all the observations on which I've taken notes throughout the years. Need I emphasise all my gratitude to the patients who have taught me my trade and made me become aware of my errors (at times serious) as well as lead the way into the labyrinth of these structures' interpretations? If I've reduced them to silence here, it is not only out of tact (but could I have said all that I think about them?); it is, further, because I preferred to let my memory work over my experience with them or, in some cases, with those who still carry on their experience with me, in pursuit of the *Durcharbeitung*.

Whatever it takes, however, I must resolve to draw this reflection to a close. I've tried to clarify to the greatest extent possible the evolution of Freud's thinking, which led him to sum up in the way he argued. I then tried to understand how his legacy was taken up by others, that is, how the differing angles on his thinking, from Melanie Klein to Winnicott, were construed. French writers have provided new perspectives on the role of the signifier in the theory and have opened up the pathways of psychosomatics and psycho-criminology, in addition to works which are more directly inspired by "classic" psychoanalytic clinical practice.

Ultimately, I'd like to think of this essay as an extension of *The Work of the Negative* (Green, 1993), its implementation starting out from a problem about which, beginning in 1920, a great deal of ink has been spilled and still more will surely be spilt. Nothing is more difficult than getting a patient to admit the existence of unconscious pleasure in pain. And if I've very much struggled in writing this book, I've gotten a great deal of pleasure out of it thanks to those who have encouraged me to pursue my reflection. Perhaps one will say, just as it was said about Freud, that these ideas have come about due to a wearing down by age. So be it.

References

Ameisen, J. C. (1999). *La sculpture du vivant: le suicide cellulaire et la mort créatrice* [*The Sculpture of Living Things: Cell Suicide and Creative Death*]. Paris: Le Seuil.

Balier, C. (1996). *Psychanalyse des comportements sexuels violents* [*Psychoanalysis of Violent Sexual Behaviour*]. Paris: Presses universitaires de France.

Balier, C. (Ed.) (2005). *La violence en abyme* [*Violence within Violence*]. A. Green (Pref.). Paris: Presses universitaires de France.

Barnes, J. (2001). *Early Greek Philosophy.* Second edition. London: Penguin.

Bergeret, J. (1984). *La violence fondamentale* [*Fundamental Violence*]. Paris: Dunod.

Bion, W. R. (1959). Attacks on linking. In: C. Mawson (Ed.), *Second Thoughts: Selected Papers on Psycho-Analysis. The Collected Works of W. R. Bion* (volume 6) (pp. 138–152). London: Karnac, 2014.

Bion, W. R. (1962). A theory of thinking. In: C. Mawson (Ed.), *Second Thoughts: Selected Papers on Psycho-Analysis. The Collected Works of W. R. Bion* (volume 6) (pp. 153–161). London: Karnac, 2014.

Bollack, J. (1965–1969). *Empédocle* [*Empedocles*]. Paris: Minuit/Gallimard, 1992.

Botella, C., & Botella, S. (2001). *La figurabilité psychique* [*Psychic Figurability*]. Lausanne and Paris: Delachaux et Niestlé.

Bott Spillius, E. (1988). *Melanie Klein Today: Mainly Theory* (volume 1) and *Mainly Practice* (volume 2). London and New York: Routledge.

Brusset, B. (1977). *L'assiette et le miroir* [*The Plate and the Mirror*]. Toulouse: Privat.

Burnet, J. (1920). *Early Greek Philosophy*. Third edition. London: Adam & Charles Black.

Cahn, R. (1983). Le procès du cadre ou la passion de Ferenczi [The trial of the frame or the passion of Ferenczi]. *Revue française de psychanalyse, 47*(5): 1107–1133.

Cassé, M. (1999). Le cosmos, conceptions et hypothèses [The cosmos, concepts, and hypotheses]. In: E. Morin & F. Morin (Eds.), *Relier les connaissances: Le défi du XXIe siècle* [*Interlinking Knowledge: The Challenge of the Twenty-First Century*] (pp. 26–32). Paris: Le Seuil.

Combe, C. (2002). *Soigner l'anorexie* [*Treating Anorexia*]. Paris: Dunod.

Davis, M., & Wallbridge, D. (1981). *Boundary and Space: An Introduction to the Work of D. W. Winnicott*. London: Karnac.

Diatkine, G. (2000). Le surmoi culturel [The cultural superego]. *Revue française de psychanalyse, 65*(5): 1523–1588.

Donnet, J.-L. (1995). *Surmoi: le concept freudien et la règle fondamentale* [*The Superego: The Freudian Concept and the Fundamental Rule*]. Paris: Presses universitaires de France.

Donnet, J.-L. (1998). Processus culturel et sublimation [Cultural process and sublimation]. *Revue française de psychanalyse, 62*(4): 1053–1067.

Donnet, J.-L., & Green, A. (1973). *L'enfant de ça. Psychanalyse d'un entretien: la psychose blanche* [*The Child of That: Psychoanalysis of an Interview: Blank Psychosis*]. Paris: Minuit.

Donnet, J.-L., & Zaltzman, N. (2003). Travail de la culture, travail de la cure [Culture-work, cure-work]. In: A. Green (Ed.), *Le travail psychanalytique* [*Psychoanalytic Work*] (pp. 211–239). Paris: Presses universitaires de France.

Dupont, J. (1988). Introduction. In: *The Clinical Diary of Sándor Ferenczi* (pp. xi–xxvii). Cambridge, MA: Harvard University Press.

Durkheim, E. (1897). *Le suicide* [*Suicide*]. Paris: Presses universitaires de France, 2004.

Edelman, G. M. (1992). *Bright Air, Brilliant Fire: On the Matter of the Mind*. New York: Basic Books.

Edelman, G. (2004). *Wider than the Sky: The Phenomenal Gift of Consciousness*. New Haven: Yale University Press.

Edelman, G. M., & Tononi, G. (2000). *A Universe of Consciousness: How Matter Becomes Imagination*. New York: Basic Books.

Enriquez, M. (1984). *Aux carrefours de la haine* [*At Hatred's Crossroads*]. Paris: Desclée de Brouwer.

Ferenczi, S. (1932). *The Clinical Diary*. J. Dupont (Ed.), M. Balint & N. Zarday Jackson (Trans.). Cambridge, MA: Harvard University Press, 1988.

Ferenczi, S., & Rank, O. (1924). *The Development of Psycho-Analysis*. Caroline Newton (Trans.). New York: Nervous and Mental Disease Publishing.

Freud, S. (1897). Letter of 21 September 1897. In: Jeffrey Moussaieff Masson (Trans. and Ed.), *The Complete Letters of Sigmund Freud to Wilhelm Fliess, 1887–1904* (pp. 264–267). Cambridge, MA: The Belknap Press of Harvard University Press, 1985.

Freud, S. (1893). Charcot. *S. E., 3*: 11–23. London: Hogarth and the Institute of Psycho-Analysis.

Freud, S. (1905). *Three Essays on the Theory of Sexuality. S. E., 7*: 130–243. London: Hogarth and the Institute of Psycho-Analysis.

Freud, S. (1913). On beginning the treatment (Further recommendations of the technique of psycho-analysis). *S. E., 12*: 123–144. London: Hogarth and the Institute of Psycho-Analysis.

Freud, S. (1915a). Instincts and their vicissitudes. *S. E., 14*: 117–140. London: Hogarth and the Institute of Psycho-Analysis.

Freud, S. (1915b). Thoughts for the times on war and death. *S. E., 14*: 275–300. London: Hogarth and the Institute of Psycho-Analysis.

Freud, S. (1917). Mourning and melancholia. *S. E., 14*: 237–258. London: Hogarth and the Institute of Psycho-Analysis.

Freud, S. (1919). The "uncanny". *S. E., 17*: 219–256. London: Hogarth and the Institute of Psycho-Analysis.

Freud, S. (1920). *Beyond the Pleasure Principle. S. E., 18*: 7–64. London: Hogarth and the Institute of Psycho-Analysis.

Freud, S. (1923). *The Ego and the Id. S. E., 19*: 1–66. London: Hogarth and the Institute of Psycho-Analysis.

Freud, S. (1924). The economic problem of masochism. *S. E., 19*: 159–170. London: Hogarth and the Institute of Psycho-Analysis.

Freud, S. (1926). *Inhibitions, Symptoms and Anxiety. S. E., 20*: 87–172. London: Hogarth and the Institute of Psycho-Analysis.

Freud, S. (1927). *The Future of an Illusion. S. E., 21*: 5–56. London: Hogarth and the Institute of Psycho-Analysis.

Freud, S. (1930). *Civilization and Its Discontents. S. E., 21*: 64–145. London: Hogarth and the Institute of Psycho-Analysis.

Freud, S. (1937). Analysis terminable and interminable. *S. E., 23*: 211–254. London: Hogarth and the Institute of Psycho-Analysis.

Freud, S. (1939). *Moses and Monotheism. S. E., 23*: 6–137. London: Hogarth and the Institute of Psycho-Analysis.

Freud, S. (1950). Project for a scientific psychology. *S. E., 1*: 295–397. London: Hogarth and the Institute of Psycho-Analysis.

Freud, S., & K. Abraham (1965). *A Psycho-Analytic Dialogue: The Letters of Sigmund Freud and Karl Abraham, 1907–1926*. In: H. C. Abraham & E. L. Freud (Eds.), B. Marsh & H. C. Abraham (Trans.). London: Hogarth and the Institute of Psycho-Analysis.

Glover, E. (1945). Examination of the Klein system of child psychology. *The Psychoanalytic Study of the Child, 1*: 75–118.

Godelier, M. (2004). *Métamorphoses de la parenté* [*Metamorphoses of Kinship*]. Paris: Fayard.

Gomperz, T. (1901). *Greek Thinkers: A History of Ancient Philosophy*. L. Magnus (Trans.). London: John Murray.

Green, A. (1973). *Le discours vivant* [*Living Speech*]. Paris: Presses universitaires de France.

Green, A. (1980). La mère morte [The dead mother]. In: *Narcissisme de vie, narcissisme de mort* [*Life Narcissism, Death Narcissism*] (pp. 222–253). Paris: Minuit. Green, 1983.

Green, A. (1983). *Narcissisme de vie, narcissisme de mort* [*Life Narcissism, Death Narcissism*]. Paris: Minuit.

Green, A. (1990). *La folie privée: psychanalyse des cas-limites* [*Private Madness: Psychoanalysis of Borderline States*]. Paris: Gallimard.

Green, A. (1993). *Le travail du négatif* [*The Work of the Negative*]. Paris: Minuit.

Green, A. (1994). Vie et mort dans l'inachèvement [Life and death in incompletion]. *Nouvelle Revue de Psychanalyse, 50*: 155–184.

Green, A. (1997). *Les chaines d'Eros: actualité du sexuel* [*The Chains of Eros: The Relevance of the Sexual*]. Paris: Odiles Jacob.

Green, A. (1999). On discriminating and not discriminating between affect and representation. *International Journal of Psychoanalysis, 80*: 277–316.

Green, A. (2000). La mort dans la vie: quelques repères pour la pulsion de mort [Death in life: Some reference points for the death drive]. In: J. Guillaumin et al., *L'invention de la pulsion de mort* [*The Invention of the Death Drive*]. Paris: Dunod.

Green, A. (2002). *La pensée clinique* [Clinical thinking]. Paris: Odile Jacob.

Green, A. (Ed.) (2003). *Le travail psychanalytique* [*Psychoanalytic Work*]. Paris: Presses universitaires de France.

Green, A. (2006a). De la psychanalyse comme psychothérapie aux psychothérapies pratiquées par les psychanalystes [From psychoanalysis as psychotherapy to psychotherapies practised by psychoanalysts]. In: Green, A. (Ed.), *Les voies nouvelles de la thérapeutique psychanalytique: le dedans et le dehors* [*New Approaches to Psychoanalytic Psychotherapy: Inside and Outside*] (pp. 13–112). Paris: Presses universitaires de France.

Green, A. (2006b). De l'inconscient au ça [From the unconscious to the id]. In: Green, A. (Ed.), *Les voies nouvelles de la thérapeutique psychanalytique: le dedans et le dehors* [*New Approaches to Psychoanalytic Psychotherapy: Inside and Outside*] (pp. 17–32). Paris: Presses universitaires de France.

Green, A. (Ed.) (2006c). *Les voies nouvelles de la thérapeutique psychanalytique: le dedans et le dehors* [*New Approaches to Psychoanalytic Psychotherapy: Inside and Outside*]. Paris: Presses universitaires de France.

Homer (1990). *The Iliad*. R. Fagles (Trans.) and B. Knox (Intro. and Notes). London: Penguin.

Jeammet, P. (2004). *Anorexie boulimie: les paradoxes de l'adolescence* [*Anorexia Bulimia: The Paradoxes of Adolescence*]. Paris: Hachette.

Kahn, L. (2005). *Faire parler le destin* [*Speak, Destiny*]. Paris: Klincksieck.

Kahn, L. (2022). Personal communication.

Klein, M. (1932a). *The Psychoanalysis of Children*. A. Strachey (Trans.). London: Hogarth and the Institute of Psycho-Analysis, 1954.

Klein, M. (1932b). Early stages of the Oedipus conflict and of super-ego formation. In: A. Strachey (Trans.), *The Psychoanalysis of Children*. London: Hogarth and the Institute of Psycho-Analysis, 1954.

Klein, M. (1946). Notes on some schizoid mechanisms. In: J. Riviere (Ed.), E. Jones (Pref.), *Developments in Psychoanalysis* (pp. 292–320). London: Hogarth and the Institute of Psycho-Analysis, 1952.

Kojève, A. (1968). *Essai d'une histoire raisonnée de la philosophie païenne* [*Essay on a Reasoned History of Pagan Philosophy*]. Volume 1. Paris: Gallimard.

Marty, P., & de M'Uzan, M. (1962). La pensée opératoire [Operational thinking]. *Revue française de psychanalyse, 27*(5): 345–356.

Marty, P., de M'Uzan, M., & David, C. (1963). *L'investigation psychosomatique* [*Psychosomatic Investigation*]. Paris: Presses universitaires de France.

de Montaigne, M. (1603). That to philosophize is to learn how to die. In: S. Greenblatt and P.G. Platt (Eds.), *Shakespeare's Montaigne: The Florio Translation of the Essays, a Selection* (pp. 13–33). New York: New York Review Books, 2014.

Morin, E., & Morin, F. (Eds.) (1999). *Relier les connaissances: Le défi du XXe siècle* [*Interlinking Knowledge: The Challenge of the Twenty-First Century*]. Paris: Le Seuil.

Perelberg, R. J. (Ed.) (1999). *Psychoanalytic Understanding of Violence and Suicide.* L. Shengold (Fore.), R. Britton (Pref.). London and New York: Routledge.

Rosenberg, B. (1999). *Masochisme mortifère et masochisme gardien de la vie* [*Deadly Masochism and Life-Guardian Masochism*]. Paris: Presses universitaires de France.

Roussillon, R. (2005). La "conversation" psychanalytique: un divan en latence [The psychoanalytic "conversation": A couch in latency]. *Revue française de psychanalyse, 69*(2): 365–382.

Schmidt-Hellerau, C. (2000). *Pulsion de vie, pulsion de mort* [*Life Drive, Death Drive*]. Lausanne and Paris: Delachaux et Niestlé.

Sifneos, P. (1975). Problems of psychotherapy of patients with alexithymic characteristics and physical disease. *Psychotherapy and Psychosomatics, 26*(2): 65–70.

Smadja, C. (2011). Le travail de psychisation du corps [The body's work of psychisation]. *Revue française de psychosomatique, 39*: 147–161.

Valabrega, J.-P. (1980). *Phantasme, mythe, corps et sens* [*Fantasy, Myth, Body, and Meaning*]. Paris: Payot.

Winnicott, D. W. (1988). *Human Nature.* London: Free Association.

Wittgenstein, L. (1971). *Tractatus Logico-Philosophicus.* German text with English translation. D. F. Pears & B. F. McGuinness (Trans.), B. Russell (Intro.). London: Routledge & Kegan Paul.

Yerushalmi, Y. H. (1991). *Freud's Moses: Judaism Terminable and Interminable.* New Haven, CT: Yale University Press.

Index

Indexer: Dr Laurence Errington
Note: (fn) indicates footnote